CU00662319

Mike Phillips

From Priest to Pastor

A Catholic Priest Pivots in Midstream

Copyright © 2023 by Mike Phillips

All rights reserved. No part of this book may be reproduced or used in any manner without written permission of the copyright owner except for the use of quotations in a book review.

FIRST EDITION

978-1-80541-006-5 (paperback)
978-1-80541-007-2 (eBook)

CONTENTS

ACKNOWLEDGEMENTS

This book has personal recollections of events and developments that led to my decision to leave the Catholic priesthood and how I transitioned into the Pentecostal ministry. In some respects, the recollections of others may differ from mine. My recollections are imperfect, but I share them truthfully to the best of my knowledge and belief. I have taken steps to protect identities.

This memoir is a lifetime of thoughts and experiences. Many people have contributed to this process, especially my parents in the early years. I owe a huge debt of gratitude to my wife Liz, who has always supported me throughout this rollercoaster ride. My children Rachael and Daniel have been patient as we walked the difficult path of leading a Pentecostal church for twenty-five years. My sister Noreen has been a great support and has never judged or criticised me.

My sincere thanks to Paul and Jill Johnson who took me under their wing when I retired from the priesthood in 1984. John Pettifor and David Shearman mentored Liz and me in ministry over the many years we knew them. Without these wonderful people, it would not have been easy for me to get out of the black hole of despair I found myself in.

I would like to thank all the people who have supported me. I appreciate the help of the people in my home Parish in Ireland. I will always cherish what you have done. The Society of African Missions has been there for me in good times and bad, helping me when I needed it most. I love the way the members of Lifespring church embraced the vision we proposed and ran with it over the years. Thank you.

Finally, I would like to thank Pastor David Littlewood and Dr Steven Jenkins who read the first draft of this book and Catherine Northey who proofread the last version. All gave me valuable comments and suggestions as I worked to put my story in writing.

Mike Phillips, Ollerton, 2023.

FORWARD

A fascinating memoir, full of emotion. I would expect nothing less from Mike, an honourable, intelligent, honest man of God. I have observed his journey for more than three decades and celebrate the evidence of the grace of God in a man who loves the presence of God expressed by his love for people.

When someone's life is encapsulated by Robert Frost's phrase, a road "*less travelled by*," what they say is probably worthy of our attention. It is wisdom to learn from those honest enough to write about "*the course corrections*" they made "*to restore balance*" to their lives. It is especially true when their theology, transformed by a revelation, changes their understanding of biblical truth. It means that Paul's words "*It is for freedom that Christ has set us free*" (Gal 5:1) have become experientially true for Mike Phillips.

From Priest to Pastor is such a book. It may save some a wasted journey down the wrong path. It may give others the courage to realise they are on the wrong path and make a brave course correction. It can help all who read it understand, for the first time or afresh, the power that is released when God speaks to us through the pages of Holy Scripture by the power of His Spirit.

However Mike's journey touches you, please be thankful that an honest man has had the courage of his convictions, making the move from priest to pastor, being vulnerable to express both pain and joy and the `guts` to write it all down.

David Shearman, Nottingham, 2023

INTRODUCTION

"It was not best to swap horses when crossing streams."[1]

When I stood before the altar to say my first Mass on 10 June 1977, it never occurred to me that one day I would have to choose between my true convictions and the beliefs and practices of the Catholic Church. It never dawned on me that I would write this book about my break with the priesthood.

Six years later in 1983, there was a defining moment in my relationship with Catholicism. A brief conversation with a senior churchman took place in a private room. I remember being bludgeoned by his words and taken by storm. When he left, the immediate effect on me was traumatic and it is no exaggeration to say that it was life-defining.

When you are brought up Catholic from childhood, you acquire an emotional and spiritual attachment to the Church. Catholic beliefs and practices are repeated and reinforced with such regularity and potency that they are ingrained into your soul. The imposing character of the institution, the towering church buildings, the paramount influence of priests and bishops in Irish society, all helped to cement the impression of the pre-eminence of the Catholic faith in the mind of a receptive child. On the day of my ordination, while I had many questions and misgivings and I believed that the

---

1 Abraham Lincoln, from the Evening Star (Washington, D.C.) – 9th June 1864.

Church was an imperfect organisation, it was inconceivable that I would break that bond.

"It was not best to swap horses when crossing streams," Abraham Lincoln once quoted an old Dutch farmer. As far as priesthood is concerned, one does not consciously set out to *"swap horses"* but on rare occasions, it does happen, and it is never easy to make such a venturesome change. The switch for me did not take place on the riverbank or in the shallows, but in the churning currents of midstream.

My main concern in leaving was not to get married. My main concern was to get well. The end of my dream was the worst thing that could happen to me, and I had to accept that the road back to well-being would be long and difficult. So, while my desire to get married was at the back of my mind, it was not top of my list.

Of course, there is always a back story to every break-up. Over the years as a trainee and then as an ordained priest, I developed doubts and misgivings about the Church, and towards the end I became very restless and disillusioned with my role. However, I was much more interested in reforming the Church from within than protesting it from outside. In this respect, my focus was to take steps in the direction of Church renewal. But then there was what I call 'the tipping point.' It was this incident with the senior churchman that made me throw in the towel more quickly than my reservations about the Church.

Today I am happily married and enjoying working in my new 'Free Church' environment. I have made the transition from priest to pastor, albeit a pastor with Evangelical, Pentecostal, and Sacramental emphases.

"I've looked at life from both sides now,"[2] quoting the words from the Joni Mitchell song. If you do not allow what has happened to you to influence your perspective, you will find that *"Success is not final, failure is not fatal – it's the courage to go on that counts."*[3]

I am a passionate believer in loyalty and faithfulness and an ardent advocate of long-term relationships, whether in marriage or in the Church. Break-ups of any kind are not my cup of tea. Given my belief in commitment, how did I end up in this quagmire of shattered childhood dreams and what positive steps have I taken to regain my mental balance and spiritual well-being?

I have delayed drafting this book for decades until the time was right. I share my memories and my present attitudes and thoughts about them long after the events because I did not want anyone to "Cry Me a River."[4]

This book reflects an inner journey along a path *"less travelled by."* While there are many who leave the priesthood, there are few who transition into the Pentecostal ministry. In this book I try to answer some puzzling questions about my life. The book explores the question of why I became a priest in the first place. What was so messed up about me and the Church that my life 'went down the drain'? What course corrections have I made to restore balance to my life? In addition, it is important to have a theology or rationale for leaving.

---

2 *"Both Sides, Now"* is a song by Canadian singer-songwriter Joni Mitchell. First recorded by Judy Collins, it appeared on the US singles chart during the autumn of 1968.

3 This quote has been attributed to Winston Churchill, although there is no evidence that he ever said it.

4 Justin Timberlake

As I explore these questions, I will outline my answers, some of which I expected and some of which were even new to me.

CHAPTER 1

IN THE BEGINNING

"Ask the former generation and find out what their ancestors learned."[5]

When I arrived at Maynooth Seminary in September 1970, there were over six hundred students. In that year, there were almost fifty seminaries open in Ireland to train young men for the priesthood. You could say the numbers joining up were phenomenal.

Through the influence of the Catholic Church, I was caught up in a wave of altruism and goodwill that swept the country. On the surface, apart from the government, the main agent of doing good was the Church. But how did this come about? What triggered this wave of altruism in the 1960s and 1970s?

My great-grandmother was born in 1845, the year the famine broke out, and she experienced what I can only describe as an apocalyptic nightmare. When I found out about her and studied the background circumstances, I could only conclude that her life is representative of the worst that the Irish people went through in those years. Like anyone else, I can so easily be inoculated against the suffering of others, but when I understand what happened in Ireland in those years, I can only react with horror and disgust.

---

5 Job 8:8

In the 19th century, virginity was highly prized by Irish society. Unmarried mothers were subject to hatred and cruel treatment by those around them. Dr Kirwan reporting to His Majesty's Commissioners in 1835 said, "... *the woman who has lost her virtue, unless repaired by a subsequent marriage, loses with it, for life, her character, and her caste.*"[6]

The scene is the Limerick workhouse, and it is Sunday afternoon, late 1872. A group of women are standing in the corner of the long hall. My great-grandmother, Johana Phillips, is one of them. She is holding her baby, Martin, born out of wedlock on 18 October 1872. The women and their babies are on display for all visitors to see. However, it is not a competition to see who the cutest baby is or who will steal the show. It is a name and shame exhibition. Johana could feel the cold kiss of a judgemental Church on her forehead. The shame these women felt was palpable. The nuns who took over the workhouse in 1861 wanted to publicly portray their 'depravity' as irresponsible, delinquent, and immoral. Johana was confronted with a Church that was not aligned with the teachings of Christ.

Famine

Johana had no choice but to go to the workhouse not only because of the unforgiving attitudes of Church and Society, but also because of the merciless economic conditions. These included poverty, famine, and eviction from people's homes.

---

6 *His Majesty's Commissioners for Inquiring into The Condition of The Poorer Classes in Ireland*, With Appendix (A.) And Supplement, digitised by the University of Southampton Library Digitisation Unit https://archive.org/stream/op1245191-1001/op1245191-1001_djvu.txt, 8 July 1835.

Before the famine, His Majesty's Commissioners were so shocked that their report in 1838 said it could not describe the living conditions that ordinary people endured. The report found that in many areas the only food was the potato. The cabins seldom supplied shelter from the weather. A bed or blanket was a rare luxury, and in almost all cases a pig and a dunghill were their only possessions. Many people were reduced to begging. "*Myself and my children are so naked, that when we go out to beg we take the blanket out to shelter us: the wetter the day the more we want it; and when we come home at night, we have nothing else to cover us,*"[7] one such lady from Ballina testified to the Commission.

In view of these terrible living conditions there was an apocalypse on the horizon. Indeed, in 1845, the same year Johana was born, a great famine occurred. Over the next seven years, the conditions listed by the Commission continued to worsen. An ugly disease attacked the potato crops. It soon spread all over Ireland.

We can only imagine the consternation and desperation of the people. The dying began with the children and then the old people. Tales of misery rolled in and with each passing day came new horror stories about the plight of the Irish. In December 1846, a reporter from the Cork Examiner visited Skibbereen.[8] He was shocked at the sight. He saw the remains of children being placed in hastily dug shallow graves with no cover or coffin. He saw wives unable to get coffins in which to bury their husbands. It was said that

7 *His Majesty's Commissioners for Inquiring into The Condition of The Poorer Classes in Ireland,* with Appendix (A.) and Supplement, (digitised by the University of Southampton Library Digitisation Unit, https://archive.org/stream/op1245191-1001/op1245191-1001_djvu.txt, 8 July 1835)

8 Ian Maxwell, *Everyday Life in 19th Century Ireland* (Kindle), p.102

every field quickly became a graveyard. Bodies lay in empty huts for days. Nameless and unattended bodies lay ignored by the roadside.

While travelling near Bantry Bay, a clergyman named John East was horrified to hear stories of wild dogs feeding on the dead bodies. These bodies *were often laid to rest uncoffined and covered with a little earth. Hence the half-starved dogs, having tasted human carrion, are becoming insatiably eager for the horrid food,*[9] the clergyman reported.

One million people starved to death during the famine. Another million fled the country. Many people boarded 'coffin ships' to Canada and the USA. Of the hundreds of thousands who sailed to North America in 1847, it is estimated that one in five died of disease and malnutrition.

The thing that fuels my horror and disgust is the action and attitudes of the authorities. Those in power backed this exit from the land. The ten thousand landowners who owned the whole of Ireland saw this as an opportunity to reduce overpopulation and use the land for grain production. Evictions were intended to drive out the surplus peasants, destroy the houses and make emigration the only choice. In fact, there was food in Ireland, but it was being exported even though people were starving to death.

Between 1841 and 1925, an estimated four and a half million people emigrated to other countries. These emigrants brought with them a hatred of the English, *"blaming the coloniser unjustly for deliberate genocide."*[10] I believe the famine itself was a natural event and the English were not to blame. However, the landowners and the British government, with their policy of non-interference in the market, must take much of the responsibility for how it was handled. When the British people learn of this horror story, they are as

---

9 Maxwell, *Everyday Life*, p.106
10 Sean McMahon, *A short History of Ireland* (Dublin, Mercier Press 1996), p.134

upset as everyone else. Since Ireland was still part of Britain at the time, the British government was prepared to let a million of its own citizens starve to death as the price of protecting free trade.

Evictions

The eviction of people like Johana from their homes took place every day before and after 1845. Tenants were usually made homeless because they did not pay their rents[11] or because the land owners wanted the land to grow grain. This is most likely what happened to Johana. It is possible that she was made homeless after the death of her father in 1869. When she had her baby in 1872, her mother was old or even dead. Her sister Catherine was blind, and her brother Thomas died in 1866. There is no information about William, her other brother. He was either dead or had moved to another country. The only conclusion we can draw is that Johana was on her own and had no means of support. Her only choice was the workhouse.

Workhouse

Workhouses became an important part of Irish society from 1838 onwards. Margaret Dixon McDougall after a visit to the workhouse in Manor Hamilton in 1882 was appalled by what she saw. She ran out of the workhouse and later

---

11 Maxwell, *Everyday Life*, p.50

reflected, "*I think it is hard for struggling poverty to go down so far as to take shelter in the workhouse. It must be like the bitterness of death.*"[12]

These workhouses were places of death. You had to be destitute to get in. They were the only refuge for the victims of famine and poverty. The most unfortunate people found a place there, including many decent people affected by hardship and abject poverty. The residents were often referred to as 'paupers' and were seen as outsiders in society.

Many women were rejected because they were about to give birth out of wedlock. Their only last resort was to give birth in the workhouse. Johana found herself in an extremely unfortunate situation. She had no choice but to go to the workhouse to find shelter and give birth to her child.

It is highly likely that Johana spent the rest of her life in the workhouse. According to my father, he remembers her body being removed from there in 1912 when he was six years old. We have a death certificate to support this.

Summing up

Our past experiences shape who we are. This is also true of a nation. The experiences of millions of people, such as Johana lived through, were key factors in the formation of Irish national identity between 1845 and 1921. Her life coincided with the prominence of a cold and harsh religious spirit, the introduction of the workhouse, the outbreak of famine and the cruel eviction of people from their homes. Johana's life was lived out during the darkest period of Irish history.

---

12 Maxwell, *Everyday Life*, p.110

So, what triggered this wave of altruism in the 1960s and 1970s that swept so many like me into the priesthood? According to a 2018 CAF research project, the Irish are the most generous people in Europe and the sixth most charitable in the world. Commenting on the findings, Sir John Low, Chief Executive Officer of CAF, said: *"It is a basic human instinct to lend a helping hand and it is always amazing to see how people in countries that have suffered from conflict and natural disasters are moved to help people in need."*[13]

It is exactly because of their experiences of suffering that the Irish stand up for the afflicted. Being Irish stands for all kinds of good qualities. These include compassion, generosity, and hospitality. They display these qualities to anyone in need. This is, of course, a general statement. It does not apply to all Irish people, and it is not exclusive to the Irish. But what the CAF survey seems to suggest is that these qualities are found more in people like the Irish because of the suffering they have gone through.

This is my own thinking to set the scene for my history as a priest. At the time of my adolescence, I was not aware of this background story. All I knew is that I was surrounded by models of people who were giving up their lives to help others. This empathy with the afflicted was a crucial factor in inspiring many young Irish people to embrace the single life. We wanted to dedicate our lives to serving others. Our culture and character inspired by a spirit of altruism, was our motive. Of course, the life of a priest was the highest and noblest example of service and selflessness. Many who wanted to live a life of service were drawn to the priesthood.

There were many who did not become priests despite this culture of altruism. The question remains, why on earth did I decide to become a priest? The pay was low, the hours were long, and life was lonely and challenging.

---

13 Low, Sir John, *CAF Giving Index 2018*, p.4

FROM PRIEST TO PASTOR

What could motivate a seventeen-year-old to sign up to become an ordained unmarried clergyman?

CHAPTER 2

WHY ON EARTH?

"Do not despise these small beginnings."[14]

My motives and intentions may have been pure, but there were certainly things about me that were messed up that led me down this path. There are several circumstances that encouraged me to come forward. My childhood and upbringing had a strong influence on me.

Childhood

Childhood was a wonderful time for me, and I have many great memories. I had a very loving family and some particularly good friends. My mother was my best friend and the most important influence in my life. I have a sister and a brother, and we were brought up by my mother as my father worked long hours or was away in London.

However, my good memories of Irish life at that time do not represent how life was for many people. Many stories from this period include accounts of sexual abuse by clergy, forced adoptions, unregistered births and the 'mother

---

14 Zachariah 4:10

and baby' scandal. Unmarried mothers were treated cruelly, neglected by their families, or forced to give their child away.

The relationship between Church and State led to a toxic watertight culture of secrecy and deception. When the lid came off, this complicit relationship broke down and people lost their trust in the Church. Many people's lives were permanently scarred by abuse that I knew nothing about, but my happy childhood laid the foundation for my time in the priesthood.

Spiritualism

Spiritualism certainly messed with my life. My first 'call' to the priesthood had its origins in a visit to a fortune teller made by my mother before I was born. The encounter told my mother that she would have three children and that one of them would be 'a soldier for Christ.'

My mother was a spiritually oriented, religious woman. She had a strong commitment to prayer and religious practices. But she never learned that the Bible forbids any contact with people who practise things like fortune-telling. When I was still incredibly young, she announced one day that I would be a 'soldier for Christ.' I had little idea what that meant at the time. My mother, on the other hand, was convinced that I was called to the Roman Catholic priesthood. This experience with the fortune teller gave the whole idea its own momentum from then on.

The thing about visiting a psychic is that his statements about probable future events are not in line with God's plans. Fortune telling is forbidden in the Bible. God tells us what he thinks of it, *"There shall not be found among you . . . anyone who practises divination or tells fortunes or interprets omens."*[15]

So compared to God's plans, divination is false, dishonest, and worthless. It is not harmless entertainment or an alternative source of wisdom. Christians should avoid all practices that involve horoscopes, ouija boards, fortune-telling, or the study of the influence of the stars on people, the use of spells or magical powers, tarot cards, necromancy, and sorcery.

The spirit world is real, but it is not innocent. Fortune tellers may have good intentions, but the spirit behind them is not interested in truth. Their predictions are meant to deceive you and lead you down a dangerous path. Fortune telling led me down a path that caused me great harm.

Over time, I assumed that being a 'soldier for Christ' meant becoming a Catholic priest. There was no other framework with which I could understand my mother's announcement. This so-called 'reading' influenced me greatly and set the course for the future.

From a young age, I was excited about serving Christ. Unfortunately, I confused this true vocation with becoming a Catholic priest. This "vocation" to the priesthood was eagerly encouraged by my mother. I practised Mass in our living room with my siblings as parishioners. The kitchen table became the altar, a tablecloth was converted into a chasuble. Various pots and pans were used as 'sacred' vessels. I soon outgrew that, but the idea remained.

---

15 Deuteronomy 18:10

Catholic Roots

Catholicism exerted an enormous influence on me as a child. It never entered my mind to think differently from what I was told over and over again. These messages came from important people like parents, teachers and priests. We were told that the Catholic Church was the only true Church and that you could not be saved outside of it. You had to be good, or you would go to hell. The cleansing fire of Purgatory awaited you if you committed less serious sins. When we received Communion, we believed that we partook of the actual body and blood of Christ. We were taught the importance of praying through Mary and the other saints. Most notably, it was instilled in me that I would make a 'good priest.'

The importance of the priesthood was firmly fixed in my mind. I learned that it was never to be approached lightly and that it was a fearful thing to even consider a vocation to the priesthood. Ordination, it was believed, left an indelible stamp on your nature that could never be removed. A person, it was said, underwent an 'ontological' change.

It was even more unthinkable that anyone who had entered the priesthood would consider leaving. Anyone who left and married was considered a Judas or apostate, tarnishing the name of the Catholic Church. I grew up in a time when Rome did not allow exceptions for priests who wanted to marry. The Church preferred them to "*burn*" than to marry.[16] Yet at the same time, the church was turning a blind eye and covering up the large-scale abuse against children, committed by its own priests.

---

16 1 Corinthians 7:9 says it is better for a person "*to marry than to burn with passion.*"

16

All these messages can confuse the mind from the beginning, and the ideas implanted are difficult to unlearn. For me, the danger was that I was not in touch with my inner self, even if I thought I was.

To these messages, add routines and rituals, all of which strengthened my faith during my childhood and adolescence. I was thoroughly initiated into Catholicism. These messages and rituals did not always give a correct picture of who God is.

Until 1959, we lived about two miles from the church. Every Sunday we rode to Mass on a donkey and cart. One Sunday morning as we passed a neighbour's gate, the donkey got spooked by something. The donkey, who normally walked at a tedious pace, suddenly became a Formula 1 driver. He raced at high speed along the narrow, winding country lane. My mother completely lost control. Down a hill he galloped, while gaining speed. We went around a bend and over a humpback bridge without slowing down. Then we climbed steeply uphill and almost reached the top before the donkey finally ran out of breath. That was the most exciting experience of my life so far. However, I remember my mother praying earnestly to 'Jesus, Mary and Joseph,' but she certainly had nothing good to say about the 'wee donkey!'

Every Sunday morning the church was full and the faithful came to Mass dressed in their 'Sunday best.' I was moved by the ritual as the priest waved the smoking censer around the altar in a set routine. The strong aromatic and earthy smell of the incense was delightful. The smoky incense rising to heaven carried the prayers of the people to the Lord. The sound of the bells awakened us to focus on the main points of the service. We were spectators at the Mass and the priest was pre-eminent. The vestments, the sprinkling of holy water, the symbols and statues that decorated the church fascinated me. All this appealed to my senses. It told me of the majesty and existence of God, who seemed to be out there somewhere.

As a child, I was very moved by the image of the priest holding up the Communion bread during Mass so that everyone could see 'God.' The Church adopted this practice in the eleventh and twelfth centuries after the doctrine of transubstantiation took centre stage. At that time there were two opposing views in the Church. According to a long-established view, the bread and wine symbolised the body and blood of Christ.[17] The other school of thought, represented by Thomas Aquinas,[18] held that the elements were Christ's actual body and blood. Aquinas' view prevailed with the belief that the Host was 'God.' The lifting of the Host then became the climax of the Mass.

Lifting the Host was something that only the privileged were allowed to do. The priests were the aristocracy, a separate 'caste' if you like. They were somehow superior to us ordinary Catholics and they alone administered the holy things of God. They had the power to change the bread and wine into the actual body and blood of Christ. It was clear that the priest had special powers, lived a unique unmarried life, inhabited a house separate from others and dressed in a special uniform. As a young man, I was drawn to this model of priesthood or ministry. It was the only model with which I was familiar.

In my childhood we had to go to confession before we could receive Holy Communion. The Council of Trent (AD 1545-1563) required that all sins had to be told to the priest in confession with all relevant information. This meant confessing what kind of sin you had committed, how often and under what circumstances or in what context you had committed it.

---

17 Tertullian *Against Marcion,* https://www.newadvent.org/fathers/03124.htm, Book IV Chapter 40

18 Alistair E. McGrath, (Editor), *The Christian Theology Reader* (Hoboken, NJ: Blackwell Publishing, 1996), pp.562-563

Confession took place every third Saturday of the month when we went into a large wooden box where we had to confess to a priest behind a small sliding door in the wall of the box. It was dark, dingy, and claustrophobic.

We confessed the things that our parents (and God) strongly disapproved of, lying, quarrelling with your sister, impure thoughts. We were already aware that God was a harsh disciplinarian who made strict demands on us for which we were accountable. These demands changed and became more demanding as we grew older, especially when it came to sex. The priest was obliged to inquire about all the details of sexual pleasure, and this decided our image of God who had a particular dislike of sexual misdeeds. God kept an exact book of the nature and details of all our sins, which he conscientiously recorded like a good accountant.

We had not yet come to know the Jesus who loves us tenderly and unconditionally just as we are. We were certainly not aware that He desired a close personal love relationship with us and not a business-like relationship with a strict and stern bookkeeper. The caricature of God as an old man with a grey beard who wanted to punish us was commonplace. God punished us when we did something wrong, and He also 'slapped' us when we did something right – just to prevent us from becoming proud. We were never challenged to receive His love. I never even considered that receiving the personal love of God for me would change my heart and consequently my lifestyle.

Therefore, Catholicism was not a bolt-on. It was central and essential to my way of life. We were brought up with good values. But the all-encompassing teachings and attitudes of the Church crept into us and permeated every aspect of our lives. When I began to seriously question the Church, it was almost impossible for me to consider breaking away.

Three Mega Church Trends

Three mega Church trends that appeared in the Catholic Church influenced me in my youth. They were self-denial, clericalism, and celibacy.

As a young man, true religion for me was characterised by self-denial. I remember going to a place of pilgrimage called Lough Derg in County Donegal. I fasted, prayed, stayed up all night and crawled on my knees to a series of 'stations'.

I learned from an early age to have an ascetic mindset and I saw the body as unhelpful and negative. The Christian life was associated with poverty, chastity and obedience, with a life of austerity and aversion to physical pleasures. Being a priest in a local diocese would have been far too easy and comfortable. I was attracted to the hardships of missionary life.

This expression of religion has a long history in the Church. An extreme form is exemplified by a monk named Simeon the Stylite. During his time in the monastery of Teleda, Syria, AD 411, he was the subject of many complaints. Simeon stank so badly that no one dared go near him. Further investigation revealed that he had tied a rope around himself under his tunic. He pulled it so tight that his flesh was rotten. His bed was swarming with maggots. He was frighteningly close to death and was eventually expelled from the monastery. You could say he was addicted to pain and suffering. He then spent the rest of his life sitting on various pillars. The pillars, called stylites, grew progressively higher and higher. His last pillar was twenty metres high. It had a platform that was secured with a railing. It was equipped with a drainpipe so that he did not have to climb down to go to the toilet.

Simeon was the first of many Stylites who followed in the years ahead. They were the celebrities of their time. It was an excellent career for anyone who craved fame and popularity. If there had been TV back then, you might see a programme called "I'm A Stylite...Get Me Down From Here!" By all accounts, Stylites conducted extensive ministry and drew large crowds.

As a dutiful and zealous young person, I embraced the theory of this ascetic heresy. The aim of this form of religion was to attain a high spiritual state through extreme self-denial. It was believed that the more the body suffered, the more one grew in holiness and overcame animal instincts. At first, this was just a way of thinking, but it eventually had a profound effect on my life choices.

Of course, Jesus never asked his followers to beat themselves up or make their bodies suffer to grow in holiness. Catholic teaching convinces people to perform acts of penance and mortification in the belief that one can grow in holiness through self-effort. Holiness, as I later understood it, is achieved progressively in our lives when the Spirit of God enables us to change and become more like Jesus. This has nothing to do with self-effort, but with a radical, heartfelt faith in God's power.

After self-denial, clericalism was the second idea that impressed me in my childhood. Clericalism is a trend that sets up a hierarchy within the Church and makes a distinction between clergy and laity. The disproportionate respect given to clergy because of their supposed moral superiority appealed to me. The power system in which the clergy became the dispensers of grace through the sacraments was attractive.

I then learned about how this power was transmitted to priests. It's called the doctrine of 'Apostolic Succession.' Apostolic Succession is the belief in the uninterrupted transmission of spiritual power from St Peter, bishop of Rome, to every priest through the laying on of hands. Consequently, in Catholic thinking, the authority of every priest goes back to Peter, the first bishop of Rome. It is said that Jesus conferred the *"keys of the kingdom"* on him.

Then of course there was celibacy. Celibacy is a promise not to get married. When you take a promise of celibacy, there is an indirect promise to remain chaste. Being chaste means not engaging in any sexual activity. If you are married, chastity means being faithful to your spouse. If you are single, it means giving up all sexual activity.

Why would a seventeen-year-old boy with little experience of life devote himself to such a vocation? In short, I had a great desire to serve God and felt that one could only love and serve God if one were unmarried. There was a strong spirit of self-denial in me that drew me to the single life. I was influenced by the Church's teaching, which was couched in very appealing and inspiring language. I understood that a celibate priest has more freedom to love the many, not just the few. Free from the constraints of family life, I could devote all my energy and love to the flock. The Church is the Bride of Christ, and priests were urged to remain faithful to Christ with an undivided heart. It follows that a married priest could never make another person the focus of his love, because priests were spiritually married to Christ.

For one who had a genuine desire to serve God, all roads led to the priesthood. The idealistic teaching of the Church was very tempting. Of course, it was not biblical in any sense of the word. The Church paid lip service to the idea that one could serve God by serving a family.

Although I was very attracted to the single life, I had little idea of the complex list of historical issues that led to celibacy being imposed on the clergy in 1123 and again in 1139.[19] I will return to this in a later chapter.

My life was the enclosure in which these practices of self-denial, clericalism and celibacy were on a collision course without equal with the truth of

---

19 Henry C Lea, *An Historical Sketch of Sacerdotal Celibacy in the Christian Church* (Kindle), p.258

the Word of God. When the two met, there was the most profound struggle that had to be resolved. In the meantime, I was taken in by the sound bites fed to us by the Church and pressed ahead with my desire to become a priest.

A Closet Heterosexual

Catholicism in Ireland in my childhood was characterised by a sex-hostile attitude. Even within marriage, sex was regarded as 'a few moments of passing pleasure.' A woman who became pregnant outside of marriage was considered a disgrace to herself and her family, and it was common for her to be sent away until the child was born. This attitude to sex was a legacy that St Augustine (AD 354-430) left to the Church. Saint Jerome and Saint Ambrose shared and promoted similar ideas about sex and marriage.

Although, I did not know it at the time, it is important for me to say that this sex-hostile environment did not come from Jesus or the Old or New Testaments. I will trace the roots of these attitudes in a later chapter.

It is not difficult to see how all this background came to influence my thinking. I guess you could call me a 'closet heterosexual' in my teenage years. Closets are small, dark places that are considered private and can also be a place where you are trapped. I apply this meaning to myself because I was a heterosexual who was afraid to come out and admit that I was attracted to the female gender.

I grew up in a strict moral environment and we were taught to treat the other sex with utmost respect. When I put two and two together, I concluded that the safest thing to do was to stay away from them and admire them from a distance. I could not take any chances and get involved. I was a shy boy who went to an all-boys school, so I did not have much opportunity to mingle.

I went straight from school to a Roman Catholic seminary. There I had few opportunities to meet the other sex over the next eight years.

In my teenage years, my friends frequented the local dance clubs. It was not my scene, and I rarely went. Once I went because there was a young lady my age whom I fancied. You could say I carried a torch for her, and I mustered enough courage to go to the dance. I remember that all the boys were standing on one side of the hall and all the girls on the other. When the music sounded for the next dance, there was a rush across the hall. During the evening, I came to this girl first and asked her to dance.

One of my favourite songs is 'Lady in Red' by Chris de Burgh. Chris is a smooth operator. Obviously, he is incredibly good with the ladies. He sings about dancing with his lady *"cheek to cheek"* and whispering to her, *"I've never seen you looking so lovely as you did tonight. I've never seen you shine so bright."* That certainly was not me. I was as awkward as a cat on stilts! I was almost speechless and stammered a few clichés. Neither she nor anyone else ever knew how I felt. It was my secret and would remain so. I was afraid of relationships, especially those that might involve intimacy! I was content to endure the agony of admiration from afar rather than 'come out' with my true feelings. I kept this attitude towards intimacy especially during my time as a priest.

By hiding my identity, I sacrificed my deep longing for love, companionship, marriage, and children. I had the belief that the unmarried state was a better way of life, and, in any case, I was 'called' to be a priest. It never occurred to me that celibacy was not my vocation. My desire to become a priest trumped all other ambitions and I saw no other possibilities. However, I could not suppress this longing, and the desire to break out of this isolated closet of horrors kept surfacing.

While I was unable to bring myself to approach a girl, I had this fantasy of a platonic relationship with an imaginary woman. Sex was out of the question for me. The idea of a union of spirits without a union of bodies attracted me. In my view, marriage was consummated in the spirit and not by any bodily union. Somehow, I had internalised Thomas Aquinas' thirteenth-century teaching that "*a marriage without carnal relations is holier.*"[20] This very idea had already appeared in the twelfth century and was advocated by Hugh of St. Victor. He called this kind of relationship a "*Josephite*" marriage because, in his view, it was the ideal kind of marriage that Joseph had with Mary[21]. Let no one be surprised because this kind of heretical notion was present in the Church either explicitly or implicitly since the time of Augustine.

Imperceptibly, the influence of Augustine, Thomas Aquinas and others was passed on in the Church. My parents had adopted sex-hostile ideas, but they were also modelled in the culture. Parents or other people can transmit ideas directly, but ideas are also absorbed by watching other people and seeing how things are done as you grow up. I saw sex as something to be fearful of. In my eyes, it was impure and shameful, as it was in previous centuries.

I have often thought about how I was brought up in the Church's time and space in the 1950s. Ireland was a very unified society and culture at that time. It was white, English-speaking, and Catholic. The Church had an unequal amount of formal and cultural power. There was a great emphasis on accepting the teachings and attitudes of the Catholic Church. Religion was in the hearts, minds and on the lips of my parents. We inherited their

---

20 Uta Ranke-Heinemann, *Eunuchs for the Kingdom of Heaven (New York, Doubleday, 1990)*, p.195
21 Uta Ranke-Heinemann, *Eunuchs for the Kingdom of Heaven*, p.164

attitudes to authority, priests, and sexuality. This had been passed down in the Church for generations. My views on sexuality, relationships and secrecy made me an ideal candidate for the priesthood.

Passion for the Underdog

I have never fired a live bullet in my life, but if we had been there, we would have taken up arms too. At least that is how we felt. I refer to the narrative we were sold about the 1916 uprising at the GPO in Dublin and the subsequent War of Independence. The narrative of blood sacrifice left a deep impression on us, and that happened thirty to thirty-five years before I was born.

My family were staunch Fianna Fail supporters. Fianna Fail was the republican party founded in 1926 to oppose the 1921 Anglo-Irish Treaty which divided the country into North and South. In our family we were very much against the partition of the country. Padraic Pearse's 1916 Proclamation of Independence hung prominently in our home. Names like Pearce and Connolly were held in high esteem. The narrative was that these heroes had sacrificed their lives for Ireland and inspired a generation of Irish to revolt against the English.

When all this took place, my father and uncles were still boys. We heard stories about how they delivered messages for the I.R.A. (Irish Republican Army) right under the noses of the British or their agents. One of my uncles was a fantastic storyteller. I remember evenings when he would enthral us with accounts of his heroic escapades against the British. We were amazed by his bravery. Later I learned that most of his stories were a figment of his imagination.

The Black and Tans were the reserve force of the Royal Irish Constabulary recruited between 1920 and 1921 to suppress the rebellion in Ireland. Many of them were veterans of World War I and were called 'Black and Tans' because of their distinctive uniforms. In their first months in Ireland, they were not subject to strict discipline, which meant that attacks by the IRA were often met with indiscriminate attacks on locals. In 1920, the Black and Tans burned and looted many small towns and villages, including Tuam, Trim, Thurles and Templemore, Tralee, and Cork. They killed locals and murdered a Catholic priest, Father Michael Griffin, in Galway.

Although all this happened thirty years before I was born, the stories made a big impression on me. We learned of these atrocities and were also aware that the English who sent their soldiers had been causing havoc in Ireland for hundreds of years. We were all convinced that if we had been alive then, we would have taken up arms.

Ireland was an economically failed state in the 1950s and I consider myself to have been brought up in the 'backwash' of the British Empire. In certain political circles in Britain, the Empire is to be celebrated. Most British people say they are proud of the Empire and its achievements. It proved British 'exceptionalism' by ruling a quarter of the world's population and spreading its culture and ideas throughout the earth. It invested in roads and infrastructure, set up trade, schools, and hospitals. This may be seen as a good thing, but the Empire also conducted brutal campaigns to extend and keep control over nations by brute force. It extracted wealth and deprived countries of essential resources and oversaw famines. Overall, the Empire left Ireland in an impoverished state, the only country in Europe whose population was below that of 1840.

I reject the dictatorial spirit that underpins Empire, just as I reject the dominance of the Catholic Church and the control of its priests. All superpowers act in the same way to protect their privilege and territory. Because of my background, I have developed an instinctive distaste for privilege even though I enjoyed privilege as a priest. The thing about privilege is that most of us are blind to it. Once you become aware of its existence in your life, you need to do something about it. I believe that 'white privilege' exists, and that many white people deny its existence. I was blind and only realised my privileged position after I left the priesthood.

As Irish Catholics we saw an Empire exercising its authority in a brutal and overbearing manner with no concern for the local population. An example of this was the landowners, many of them absentee English, who allowed millions of people to starve or emigrate during the Great Famine of the 1840s and the half century after the famine.

'The Fields of Athenry' is a song popular among Irish rugby fans. The first verse refers to a young man called 'Michael' who was deported for the crime of stealing corn to feed his young family. This song may be fictional, but it stands for the cruelty and brutality of landowners during the potato famine:

> *"By a lonely prison wall*
> *I heard a young girl calling*
> *Michael, they are taking you away*
> *For you stole Trevelyan's corn*
> *So, the young might see the morn*
> *Now a prison ship lay waiting in the bay."*

It is no surprise that countries with large diaspora populations of Irish descendants regard the land of their ancestors with great affection. For many, Ireland is not only the home of their ancestors, but many also refer to it as a 'spiritual kingdom.' This explains why a small island on the western edge of Europe exerts such influence on the international stage.

As children growing up in the 1950s, we saw the concrete consequences of hardship and deprivation. My father, like so many other Irish before him, emigrated to 'foreign' lands. In 1957 he travelled to London to look for work because there was none in Ireland. He was part of the army of Irish workers who helped rebuild Britain after World War II. The Irish workers were extremely hard working, loyal and flexible. They had left their families behind in Ireland so they could travel from town to town as the contractor needed them.

The picture at Limerick station when we said goodbye to him is still fresh in my memory. My mother was inconsolable, and we all felt a huge void in our lives. I guess you could say we grew up in a household with only one parent. He did not return to Ireland until 1963.

I grew up in this aura of victimhood and felt inferior to our English neighbours. This victim mentality gradually gave way to a passion for the underdog, a quality a minister of religion should always have. The desire to help people is a prerequisite for a successful priest. In my training as a priest, I learned about liberation theology. Liberation theology is a Roman Catholic movement that was developed in Latin America. It aims to address the problems of poverty and social injustice as well as spiritual issues.

So, I was never in favour of a 'stand-off' relationship between the Church and the world, where the Church only preaches the 'spiritual gospel.' When I became a pastor, I found that the so-called 'fortress mentality' that has traditionally encouraged the Pentecostal Church to build its walls against an evil world empire, hold on for grim life and to pray for Jesus to deliver us, was not an idea that I adopted.

Career Choice

The community I grew up in is a lovely little village, situated on top of one of the green and lush rolling hills of the Golden Vale – the land of dairy farmers. In my family, we were working class and career opportunities had not increased since the 19th century. Fifty per cent of men and twenty-five per cent of women worked in agriculture. Life was hard and impoverished. In the 1950s, half a million people left Ireland to seek work overseas, which was sixteen per cent of the population. The country was in recession.

My father lost his job with the local farmers. It was 1950s Ireland where welfare was only paid for six months, so for him it was either leave Ireland or starve. He was forced to move to London in 1957 where he earned twelve pounds a week and worked on building projects.

Although we were born into a country with a weak and failing economy, my parents always gave us the impression that we were rich. My mother wanted her children to be educated because she did not want us to end up in the same low-paid jobs as her and my father. She was smart enough to realise that education equals greater opportunities in life. Secondary school fees cost money, but they were able to save enough to secure places for us in post primary school.

I remember one of my first days in secondary school when we were introduced to the principal. Brother Flannan was a big, strong man, and a bully. The Order of De La Salle Brothers ran a chilling disciplinary regime and I often saw boys being beaten and kicked by various teachers. You may have seen the film *Song for a Raggy Boy*, which features the same order. Most of the time I escaped the harsh discipline, but occasionally I got six strokes on both hands. Brother Flannan knew how to punish you with his long swinging bamboo cane.

There were forty students in the class from all over the district. Brother Flannan liked to speak to the pupils in Gaelic and you wanted to give him an intelligent answer when it was your turn. On the day in question, Brother Flannan went around the class asking questions in Gaelic. Due to the poor quality of teaching in my primary school, I was unfamiliar with Gaelic and had no idea what was being said. I sat in the very last row of seats. Finally, it was my turn and he asked me a question. Having no idea what he was saying, I answered 'Ta,' the only word in Gaelic I had learned in my seven years at school. The whole class burst out laughing. He must have decided that my humiliation in front of the class was sufficient punishment in this case and turned to the next pupil.

In secondary school, I did not consider myself to be exceptionally intellectually gifted. I studied hard and made steady progress in the five years I attended that school. The support of my parents gave me a reason to work hard, and I eventually graduated from secondary school with honours in Gaelic, French, English, Latin, and Geography (my favourite subject). After that, I attended various colleges and universities where I earned several degrees, including a postgraduate degree. Not bad for someone who had a dreadful start.

Along the way, a great teacher called Mrs Smith was a huge help and inspiration to me. She was enthusiastic about giving us the best chance to do something useful with our lives. Her quiet enthusiasm for her students was contagious. From day one she was tireless in helping you. A brilliant quality of hers was the meticulous way she marked your homework and although there were many of us in the class, they were returned to us the next day like clockwork. Mistakes were crossed out in red pen, but I do not remember getting less than an eight out of ten. That always spurred me on to do better next time.

Thanks to my good performance at school, I was eligible for one of the county council's coveted scholarships. With this I was able to pay my tuition fees at the university attached to the seminary. My mother also managed to source funds from the USA from a cousin named John Callahan, the only son of my mother's aunt. He was born in 1895 but had to return to Ireland in 1900 because both his parents died. He lived with my grandmother until he returned to the US in 1915. He studied law and was promoted to clerk of the Supreme Court in New York. Recognising the help he had received as an orphan, he was always willing to help our family.

As an emotionally immature teenager, I felt that belonging to the clergy would give me a sense of importance and privilege. Looking around my small village, the priesthood was the most attractive choice for a challenging and useful life, and it was the best choice for being someone in life, not a nobody. However, I never thought of it as a career ladder. For me it was more of a vocation than a career.

Why enlist in the priesthood? My upbringing helped me and messed me up at the same time. Compared to others, there were people who were better at many things. But few had the same passion for religion or for the underdog. That was what you could call my 'distinctive', or as they say nowadays my 'unique selling point.' Where else could you live out that passion and desire? The Catholic priesthood was the obvious choice.

Once I decided that priesthood was right for me, there was great competition for candidates among the many dioceses and religious congregations. I had to make a choice and then I would begin my preparations for the priesthood in the seminary. Seminary life was not what I expected. My fellow students were by no means gloom mongers and we had great fun. I was also able to take advantage of the long holidays to broaden my experience.

CHAPTER 3

JOKERS AND RULE BREAKERS

"Remember, if you fail to prepare you are preparing to fail."[22]

In secondary school, the priesthood was often advertised. We had many priests from religious orders come to our school as guest speakers. Recruiters used robust language to attract candidates.[23] They would speak to our class and make their 'pitch.' A priest called Billy eventually recruited me. He had the charisma to present the unmarried life as a life without obstacles and ties. One had to be ready to be deployed anywhere in the world at a moment's notice. We would be a spiritual flying squad. He appealed to the romantic adventurer in me to be free of family ties to travel the world. He drew on the fighter in me to go forward and fight the good fight of the faith to win nations for Christ. He called out to the social worker in me who was always on the side of the outcast, the poor, and the victim. I had listened to many other 'pitches' before, but Billy's presentation at once captivated me.

---

22 Charles Clay Doyle, Wolfgang Mieder, and Fred R. Shapiro, (complied by), *The Dictionary of Modern Proverbs* (Yale University Press, New Haven, 2012), p.73

23 Thomas O'Loughlin, *The Catholic Church, and Celibacy: An Approach from Historical Theology* (The Japan Mission Journal, 2013) p.201

Seminary Life

Preparation for the priesthood, which took eight years, required attending and graduating from a seminary. Seminaries are training colleges for priests. They were set up following the Council of Trent (AD 1645-1653). This Council was an attempt to reform the Catholic Church after the Reformation. In response to the reformers and the corruption of the clergy, it was felt that the Church needed to double down on celibacy and the training of priests.

After Vatican II rules were relaxed. Nevertheless, during our preparation for the priesthood, we still lived as if in a monastery, even though lay students, including female ones, were allowed to study alongside us. While some seminarians took advantage of this, many of us held back because of our felt vocation to celibacy. Outside of this environment, we had little contact with people or parish work. It was a life of physical work (only in the first year), study, prayer and rest. In the first year we had to get up at 6.30am, wash with ice-cold water and then spend an hour in prayer. Meals were taken in silence, and we took turns reading aloud from the lives of the Society's founders. They were stories of heroism, suffering and self-denial. After breakfast, manual labour was the order of the day and my task, together with another student, was to clean the corridor leading to the rooms where the 'gods' (ordained priests) lived.

To graduate from the seminary, we had to study philosophy as well as biblical, dogmatic, moral, and pastoral theology. I studied liturgy, church history, canon law, homiletics, and missiology to get knowledge on these subjects. I also did secular studies and graduated in French and English.

When I took up my studies, I expected my fellow students to be serious and conscientious gloom-mongers. God was a serious guy and was against anyone having fun. The reality was quite different, and I met an entire range of personalities who were anything but doomsayers. To use an Irish slang expression, 'they were gas men.'[24] We had a lot of fun with mischief-makers, pranksters, tricksters, jokers, chancers and even dossers. But among them there were also those who were serious about their vocation. The craic (pronounced crack) and friendship were always accompanied by an inexhaustible supply of coffee, tea, and biscuits. In Ireland, the closeness of a relationship can be measured by how easy it is to 'slag each other off.'[25] Over time, my ascetic streak had to bow to the easy-going and fun-loving attitude of my colleagues.

At one point in my first year, the Dean of Students came back to find that someone had committed the unthinkable religious misdemeanour of putting a pipe in the mouth of the stature of the Virgin Mary. The refectory became a 'war zone' when the supervising priests took a break. The missiles were usually in the shape of wet paper serviettes.

The local pub was where the most frequent rule breakers met on Friday or Saturday nights. Although I was by no means a frequent rebel, I once found myself in front of the dean. We were sitting in the pub on a Wednesday night enjoying a quiet beer when the great man came in with some of his friends. We thought we might get away with it, but we found ourselves 'on the carpet' the next day. Of course, the most common non-conformists were never caught.

One of the best things about seminary life was the long summer holidays. I used this time every year to go to France and work for an aid organization. I learned a new language, got to know another culture, and saw the impact my contribution could make. One of my tasks was to take food to senior

24 A 'gas man' is a comedian.
25 To slag someone off means to tease, mock or poke fun at them.

citizens in Paris, most of whom lived as 'prisoners' on the sixth floor of their apartment blocks, as the buildings had no lifts.

I remember returning from Paris, probably in 1973, and landing at Dublin airport with 50p in my pocket. I hitched a lift to Limerick which was 120 miles away. The weather was atrocious and very few people were 'picking up.' By 10.30pm, I got to Portlaoise with still 60 miles to go. Whatever else happened, I had to eat, so I went to a fish and chip shop and spent the 50p. As I sat there pondering my predicament, my eye caught a B&B sign as I scanned the area. I decided to go and explain my situation and hope for mercy, promising to send the money when I got home. Thank you Mrs. Phelan for taking me in, looking after me and giving me breakfast the following morning.

I must mention the strange experience I had during the night. In pitch darkness, I was woken up as the door to my bedroom opened. I could see the silhouette of a man and I knew he was drunk. He walked round the bed and got in beside me under the blankets. I froze and don't think I slept until the sun rose. After breakfast, I was out of there as fast as I could, and I was home by 10.30am. Of course I sent the postal order for £1.25 to Mrs. Phelan. It is still a mystery as to why the drunk came and slept in my bed that night.

Diaconate

Prior to entering our final year in the seminary, we were expected to take a promise of celibacy. Simply put, celibacy is a promise not to marry. This was not a vow, but a commitment to a bishop in the Latin rite. If one is celibate in the Latin rite, it means that one may not marry, implicitly committing oneself to chastity.

It was Easter Monday 1976, and thirty-five young men were lying on the floor in front of a bishop to take a promise of celibacy. I was one of them, right in the middle of the group. We were all dressed in a long white robe called an alb. The venue for the ceremony was the exquisite college chapel at St Patrick's College in Maynooth.

This was a big step, but did I ever think of marrying and having children? The answer is 'yes', of course I did. Would I have left the seminary before I took the promise if I had met the right person? I cannot say for sure, but the answer is probably 'yes'. The closer my ordination came, the more reservations I had about celibacy. Call it revelation if you like, but I was aware that the theology of celibacy was built on a very shaky foundation. So if I had met the right person, I probably would have left the seminary. Besides my desire to work in ministry, I had a deep desire to get married.

I was able to deal with these feelings in seminary, surrounded by good friends, good conversation, sporting activities and challenging academic studies. Nevertheless, the desire to marry kept resurfacing, even though I tried hard to suppress it for a long time.

I have to go back to my fourth year of study and four years before my ordination to explain how God did something extraordinary in my life. It was a significant event because it was the catalyst that turned my world upside down and caused me to question the Church. The Holy Spirit led me to encounter the Word of God in a way that convicted me of the many unsafe practices and systems of the Church, including celibacy.

CHAPTER 4

SOMETHING EXTRAORDINARY

"Let anyone who is thirsty come to me and drink."[26]

In lay Catholic language, divine encounters are reserved for 'Holy Joes'. But on that evening in 1973, the Holy Spirit entered my experience in an amazing way. Superlatives are not enough to describe what He did for me in that encounter. This was a truly formative and life-changing meeting around which the rest of my life would revolve. I was told later that I was baptised in the Holy Spirit. I was 'born again'[27] and baptised in the Holy Spirit simultaneously. The law of God was written on my mind and hidden in my heart.[28] This was to mark my struggle in the years to come: to follow the law of God in my heart or the laws of the Catholic Church. I came to know the law of God as my inner voice.

The extraordinary encounter arose from a dinner conversation with another student named Billy, who quoted from John's Gospel: *"On the last and greatest day of the feast, Jesus stood and said in a loud voice, 'Let anyone who is thirsty come to me and drink.'"*[29]

---

26 John 7:37
27 John 3:3
28 Hebrews 8:10
29 John 7:37

Billy spoke very personally about God with a quiet passion and conviction. This contrasted with the priests in the seminary who always spoke very learnedly about God. Most of them were dry and uninteresting. God was more a subject for learned debate than a person to relate to.

Later that evening, on pondering Billy's words, something incredible and extremely powerful happened to me. A supernatural presence came over me! Heaven had just made an indescribable entrance into my life. In that moment, I met God in a way that I cannot really describe. His entrance came with a majesty that cannot be put into words. His greatness and eternal goodness seemed endless. His presence flooded me in waves, and I lost track of time. It was a spiritual washing and an energy infusion. It was a sovereign act of God. After all the years of living with the form of religion, I was finally aware of its power. In seminary my life was a spiritual wasteland, but suddenly streams of living water flowed and bubbled within me. Birds sang as never before, and nature took on a beauty not previously recognised. My life had changed irrevocably. This was a distinct experience in my life, leaving no doubt that something astonishing had happened.

I was filled with a love I had never known. That was the moment I was born again of the Spirit of God. God showered me with His incredible love and at the same time showed me His unspeakable majesty and benevolence. My chains fell off and I became a child of God. From that day on, I knew that God was real beyond any doubt. It became my burning desire to show the world that God is a reality.

Recipients of God Encounters

Why me? Why was this happening to me? In Catholicism, 'saints' were the recipients of God-encounters, and I was no saint. What made me a candidate to receive a visit from God in the heart of a Roman Catholic Seminary? The religion I knew up to that point made exceptional holiness the passport to an encounter with God. All the great saints that the Church celebrated were distinguished by an outstanding life of prayer, self-denial and a way of life totally devoted to God. Any ordinary Catholic in the pew who claimed to have had a supernatural encounter with God would be accused of arrogance. I was to learn that God had a plan and a promise *"for you and for your children and for all who are far off – for all whom the Lord our God will call."*[30] God encounters are not reserved for those who are especially holy, but for those who hunger and thirst after the Lord.

When the Spirit came on the day of Pentecost, He brought unrest and upheaval. He changed the way things had always been. He confronted the authorities of His time. He shook the roots of formalised religion, and He turned the world upside down. On the day of my personal Pentecost, the Spirit broke into my family line. Things were never to be the same again. The Spirit brought immense joy, but also turmoil and upheaval in the years to come.

---

30 Acts 2:39

A Dissident Catholic

After this experience, I became a dissident Catholic and began to question my faith. The systems of the Church no longer appealed to me. This was not something others taught me, but something I felt inside. I was caught in a dilemma between the teachings of the Church and what I now experienced. The Catholic Church did not seem to be in harmony with the New Testament. In the years that followed, the Church lacked innovative leadership and was reluctant to adapt. Most superiors rejected change, preferring either to keep the status quo or to return the Church to an earlier golden era.

Vatican II promised to open the windows of the Church and blow away the cobwebs. The Council promised a shake up, but that never really came. While many regular members were eager for change, there was little willingness among those in power for Holy Spirit-led reform. Hans Kung makes the point that within five years of Vatican II, "... *there was an ever-increasing and nervous concentration on the maintenance of the status quo and the maintenance of spiritual power, no part of which would be willingly surrendered.*"[31]

After this personal experience of God, sacraments became far less important to me. The role of the clergy as go-betweens with God no longer made a great deal of sense. There was an open heaven that all Christians could experience. Pentecost opened a whole new world of relationship with God. After my encounter, Christianity was about the Holy Spirit visiting us directly, without the help of sacraments or intermediaries. This of course is a great threat to clericalism and the priesthood.

---

31 Hans King, *Infallible?* (William Collins & Co Ltd, London, 1971), p.16

To Go or Stay?

These new insights put pressure on me to drop out of seminary and do church elsewhere. At the same time, I knew I had a real calling to ministry. My real question was, "*Am I in the right Church?*" I had to make a serious decision. Some of my colleagues left the Church and joined other Christian churches. Their choices made a strong impression on me. Others said God wanted us to stay in the Catholic Church and renew it from within. I listened to their voices and committed myself to renewing the Church from within.

In hindsight, it is easy to say that this was the wrong decision. However, I knew little about other churches and some that could have attracted me may have been correct in their theology, but I was not ready at that time to take the leap. I was under pressure to make a huge decision when I was just getting to grips with the fundamentals of Christianity.

The urge to leave the seminary remained. I once discussed these concerns with my mother. Instead of telling me, *"Mike, this is your life. I will support you no matter what you decide,"* I was met with resistance. The pressure to conform was immense and the pushback was so strong that I decided to put the decision on hold for the time being and continue my studies at the seminary.

Hail Mary Pass

But time was running out and a decision had to be made, and that is when the absurd idea came to me. This decision was bad; perhaps not as bad as Zeppelin's decision to fill the Hindenburg with hydrogen, but bad, nonetheless. About four months before my ordination, I read the Acts of the Apostles:

"*And they cast lots for them, and the lot fell on Matthias.*"[32] That was it! I got the bright idea to cast lots and follow the outcome. I drew a long straw and a short straw, and circumstances show that I drew the short straw. I rolled the dice and accepted the result to go forward for ordination.

This was a desperate last minute Hail Mary pass in the hope of success. A Hail Mary pass is an exceedingly long forward pass in American football, usually used as a last resort. According to statistics, only 9.7% of Hail Mary attempts are completed successfully.

The isolation of having to make that decision alone in those days was excruciating. I would never advise anyone to throw a Hail Mary pass in the way I did. I had eight years of preparation to change my mind, but my decision went right down to the wire.

However, as I was to find out later, celibacy was the real issue, and that horse had already bolted from the stable, since I had already made a promise a year before my ordination. In all the training and preparation, priesthood took centre stage. Ordination to the Diaconate, involving the promise of celibacy, took place without too much fuss. Unfortunately, I did not give it the importance it deserved because ordination to the priesthood was the highest prize.

In the years that followed, as I lived the life of a priest, I found that the loyalty and intense sacrifices demanded by the church clashed with the New Testament on many levels. In the next chapter I will talk about this unconditional loyalty and my life as a Catholic priest.

---

32 Acts 1:26

CHAPTER 5

UNQUALIFIED ALLEGIENCE

"...the priest must clearly understand that he belongs body and soul, with all that he is, to this church...."[33]

On my first day as a priest, I had more questions than statues dotted around the church. I asked myself, *"Am I in the right place?" "Do I really belong here?"* I had this unsettling feeling in the pit of my stomach that somehow, I was in the wrong place. There was a clear discrepancy between what I was saying outwardly and what I was feeling inwardly. However, it took me a long time to take matters back into my own hands.

Struggles and Privileges as a Priest

I hated being called 'Father.' The whole experience was difficult. It dawned on me that I would continue to struggle with my new status. Although I had no qualms about doing ministry and proclaiming the gospel, I had many questions and qualms of conscience about the context in which I was being asked to do this.

---

33 Karl Rahner, *Meditations on Priestly Life* (London, Sheed and Ward, 1973), p.101

Life as a priest does not begin until you graduate from seminary and begin to preside over Church ceremonies and lead public worship services. You begin with the administration of the sacraments of the Church and all the other rituals and duties associated with the priesthood.

I was very well looked after, especially during my seminary and priestly years. I never had to worry about where my next meal would come from, where I would sleep, how I would pay my bills or how I would get around. My travel arrangements were taken care of, my bed was made every morning, my room was cleaned, and my food was ready. It is like being a professional footballer whose every whim is catered for so he can concentrate on playing football. We were married to the Church and our only job was to take care of the spiritual needs of the Church. This was the trade-off, unqualified allegiance in exchange for total security.

Being a priest brings many daily challenges. The daily rituals of saying Mass, hearing confessions, administering other sacraments, running the parish and making an impact on people's lives are a constant occupation. In Africa, one was always pressured to be involved in building projects such as churches and schools. To accomplish this job description, you needed an entire range of personal skills and leadership qualities, most of which were not taught in the seminary.

When I was officially made a priest, to use a comparison from the Hindu class system I was translated from a lower to a higher social class. If I expected to be beamed up to a greater level of holiness, I would have been disappointed. If I had expected access to some joyous vision of angels singing the 'Hallelujah Chorus', again this would be a let-down. There was no holiness differential or communication hot line. On the plus side, I did receive more female attention and you were allowed to jump queues because you were perceived to be about such important business. People did tend to show you more respect. Police let you off with minor violations or infringements. *"Be more careful in future Father. Off you go now."*

It was strange how people began to act differently towards me. They went into 'priest mode' when they met me, like the married couple in the sitcom *Father Ted*. This couple hated each other's guts and argued constantly but in an amazing and unexplainable way went through an attitude transplant when Father Ted appeared. One local gentleman, a little older than me, congratulated me and seemed honoured by the fact that on one occasion we had a fistfight. Others tipped their hats on meeting me. Some were bringing me money to 'say a Mass' for the dead or asking me to come to their home to say Mass.

Undoubtedly, there was an addiction to be had from the power, influence, and respect that you gain from being male and unmarried. As a priest, I experienced the admiration and reverence that many people, especially women, showed me. Over time, one gets used to this respect. The cult of clericalism and the power that comes with it is at the heart of many problems in the Church. The privilege of clericalism allows a paedophile priest, for example, to continue to stand at the altar, but excommunicates a godly woman who tries to do so.

Absolute Loyalty

Karl Rahner articulates it well when he says that as a priest you bury yourself, your personality, your centre into a pre-programmed system. *"...the priest must clearly understand that he belongs body and soul, with all that he is, to this church, to her task, to her mission, her work, her destiny, and can never dissociate himself from these things.*"[34] By proclaiming the priesthood as a *"pre-programmed"* system, Rahner affirms the roboticisation of the ministry. It is as if the priest is an automated machine that can carry out certain tasks according to a programme set by others. The religious structure makes an absolute claim on you. You owe the Church your absolute loyalty to act according to an almost robotic system. That was not my style, and it was certainly not the style of the pastors and ministers of the New Testament.

A priest can experience a wide range of emotions in a single day. Some days you sail through calm waters, while other days you feel like you are in the middle of a perfect storm. On rare occasions, you experience immense joy when you help someone receive God's forgiveness. On other occasions, you are frustrated because you know that confession is merely a ritual for many people. Even if someone has confessed to a heinous crime, e.g., murder or sexual abuse of children, Canon Law does not allow a priest to tell the authorities anything that people shared in the confessional. The priest can of course refuse absolution to someone until he has confessed the crime to the authorities. Excommunication follows automatically if a priest breaks the seal of confession.

The ideal Catholic priest must have huge emotional resilience and be skilled and knowledgeable in a wide range of areas and subjects. Like most ideals, it is impossible to achieve. The thinking is that any man who puts himself forward for such a role while denying himself the support of a companion, deserves the highest regard and is placed on a pedestal.

For me, it was very problematic to belong to a pre-programmed system. The priesthood was like an assembly line. I was involved as a priest, but

---

34 Karl Rahner, *Meditations on Priestly Life* (London, Sheed and Ward, 1973), p.101

only to 'automatically' perform certain actions and rituals as you said certain predetermined prayers and words. You accepted, by default, a system set by others and was never encouraged to be imaginative or creative. The Holy Spirit was not given freedom to move through the gifts of either the clergy or the laity.

The Lord, on the other hand, never gave this task to a single unmarried man. As early as the third century, the Church began to shift away from being a community that drew on the diverse skill sets of its members.[35] Instead, it adopted the flawed 'one-man band' leadership style, which places enormous strain on individual priests. Why should a single man be expected to meet the needs of his entire flock, both male and female? This struck me as an illogical and unbiblical model of Church. This should not be about releasing the few for the sake of the many but releasing the many for the sake of all.

All Christian ministry requires high levels of sacrifice, for the call of God is sacred. My discomfort with the Church went deeper than the intense sacrifices, such as celibacy and unconditional loyalty, demanded by the Church. From the moment I met God in the seminary, I felt uneasy about my commitment to the Church. The Holy Spirit began to convince me of the truth of His Word, and I began to see that these sacrifices were in conflict with the good practice of the New Testament Church. God's Word had found a home in me and would not let me go.

On the other hand, I was caught in a conflict of interest, as I did not want to cause pain to my family by leaving the seminary or the priesthood. Therefore, having cast lots concerning ordination, I was ordained priest on 9 June 1977 and then "cut my teeth" in ministry in an African rural parish.

---

35 1 Corinthians 2:12-13; Romans 12:3–5

CHAPTER 6

A PRIEST IN AFRICA

"To awaken quite alone in a strange town is one of the most pleasant sensations in the world. You are surrounded by adventure."[36]

New Things

I remember flying to Accra in September 1977 with my two colleagues – Anthony Kelly and Gus O'Driscoll. We spent the first six months in Ghana learning the language before working in the mission. It *"put me to the pin on my collar"*[37] to learn this new language because the same word in the *Twi* language can mean something different depending on the tone you use. There are many words that sound the same to an English speaker but differ only in their tone, which can be high, medium, or low. These differences make it extremely difficult for English speakers to learn and speak the language fluently.

My first parish assignment as a priest was in the middle of the forest. Since my job was to visit outstations and spend nights in the forest, I had to

---

36 Freya Stark, *Bagdad Sketches*, (2011, Tauris Parke Paperbacks)

37 This means I had to make a significant effort

put up with all kinds of miserable living conditions. The houses were built of mud with corrugated iron roofs. Some of the houses had wooden lattice ceilings. I remember something running across the ceiling in one house, which disturbed me when I tried to go to sleep. The streets were not paved, and you were sometimes up to your ankles in mud when wading through the village. There was no electricity and no running water. I had a light with me, powered by the battery of my car, so at least I could read at night. I bathed with a bucket of water, and I remember one station where I had to bathe in the open at the back of a house.

I ate everything that was made available to me, provided it was prepared with bottled water. It should be noted that the kitchens did not have five-star hygiene ratings. Everywhere in this part of West Africa there is a dish called 'fufu.' It is made from a mixture of pounded cassava or yam and plantain. The mixture is pounded by hand until it has the consistency of sticky mashed potato.

When I visited people's homes in the late afternoon, I often felt like a pied piper, for all the children followed me around. A very distinctive sound was the pulsating 'thump, thump, thump' of pestle on mortar. As I got closer, I saw two people, usually women, one of whom was standing and rhythmically pounding with a long pestle. The other person was seated with her hand in the mortar. She was turning and whipping the mixture with agile hands and remarkable precision, while adding a little water now and then. They always invited me to eat with them. I did not usually eat fufu unless I was sure it had been prepared with purified water. In the villages, I was usually offered 'ampesi.' This is a meal served with cocoa-yam leaves called 'kontomire.'

The living conditions did not really bother me. They were part of the job. What bothered me, however, was the enormous challenge of caring for so many churches and the fact that I was expected to grow people to maturity in Christ without the support of other gifted people around me.

Risk and Danger

I remember an occasion when I experienced a sudden surge of energy and my heart beat faster while my brain became more alert. It began quite innocently. I heard something coming into my room, but I did not see it. Many people I met were afraid to travel to Africa because there are wild animals and reptiles. They told me they would freak out at the thought of the bugs, snakes and animals. But that's what I signed up for, the excitement, the danger, the challenge and the difficult living conditions.

Reality struck home when a snake slid into my room. Most snakes that invade homes are small, but this one was a beast, and most snakes in Ghana are venomous and deadly. I knew enough not to go up against it alone. It was at least three metres long and was looking for water or food, because snakes avoid humans whenever possible.

It was a beautiful, peaceful morning at the mission station, and the seclusion gave me an opportunity to sit at my desk and write some letters. The door was open and a light refreshing breeze was blowing through the room. As I was busy writing, I barely heard the shuffling sound on the floor. I ignored it, thinking it was just a piece of paper gently blowing in the wind. The persistent noise eventually caught my attention and when I looked over, there was a tail disappearing under a cupboard. It did not bother me because I assumed it was a lizard, and lizards were both harmless and plentiful. I bent down to look more closely and noticed this large object curled up under the

cupboard. Of course, I was cool as a cucumber and brave as a lion! I ran out
of the house and into the school next door.

Mr Agyei, the teacher, came with a long pole, the tool all professionals
need in this situation. In Ghana, it was not customary to release such snakes
back into the wild. I will therefore not go into detail about how the snake was
dispatched, but only say that it needed the help of a broom, which I was able
to provide. Later, when I thought about it, I realised how vulnerable I was.
I shudder to think what would have happen if the snake had come my way.

My fridge in the mission house was not properly sealed and I often discovered cockroaches in it. After spending a few years in Africa and living in
unhealthy living conditions, you become careless about your surroundings
and even your health. In the autumn of 1980, I was diagnosed with hepatitis
A, a liver disease. Six weeks at Akwatia Hospital in eastern Ghana gave me
many opportunities to rest, pray and play with the hospital cat.

During my time in language school, I almost died or at least I thought I
was dying. The poor living conditions are particularly conducive to illness,
and I was not immune to the effects of these conditions. One morning I
woke up with a severe headache, drenched in sweat and with an extremely
high fever. It felt like a near-death experience. I had this excruciating pain
in my lower back and could not turn over in bed. When I finally managed
to get up, I was staggering like a drunk. I at once suspected it was malaria,
which is caused by mosquitoes. At least I hoped it was not something worse.

Over the next few days, I took medication and waited for the fever to go
down. This was followed by a bout of depression that weakened me. I was
told this was normal, but it made me question my whole existence. What
was I doing here in the first place? Did my life or ministry have any meaning
at all? It was a truly horrible experience, accompanied by a brutal attack of
homesickness. Every time I came down with malaria, the frequent fever and

subsequent depression were followed by a profound sense of gratitude that it was over.

Testing and Temptation

The party in front of the mission station had been in full swing for hours. The crickets never seemed to tire of rubbing their wings together and making their characteristic chirping sound in search of a mate. The sound of the crickets did not dampen the sound of the generator which was humming away in the background. There was no air conditioning, and the room was hot and stuffy.

There was the usual 'knock' on the door. This was not a knock in our sense of the word, but a vocal sound – 'kokooko' – a signal that someone was coming in. A lady dressed in traditional dress appeared at the door. She was one of the women who cooked my meals when I visited one of the rural villages. It would be rude to refuse her entry, but it was unusual and already late in the evening. However, as I recognised her, I allowed her to enter.

We followed the usual Akan ritual of shaking hands and then asked her to sit down. *"Would you like some water?"* was the next question. Then, as the custom dictates, you ask, *"Why have you come?"* *"I just came to see you,"* she replied. This was awkward and some small talk ensued. Since she did not speak much English, the conversation was in the local language. Finally, she signalled to go to the bedroom. It was at this point that the penny dropped, *"Why should we do that? I am a celibate priest,"* I said. I explained to her that I could not comply with her request and suggested that she leave. Her reluctance was obvious, and her protests were unmistakable, and I hurt her feelings. I had to go to the door, hold it open, and ask her to leave. Even the threat of calling the caretaker (who lived next door) did not completely convince her. Eventually she understood the message and left, albeit reluctantly.

This kind of offer is easy to refuse. It is much more difficult to deal with a relationship where you fall in love with someone. That is much more problematic. I could be wrong, but that happens to most priests. As I said before, human impulses do not surrender just because you wear a Roman or clerical collar.

In a sense I can say, without being arrogant, 'I am every priest.' By this I mean that my story is not atypical of what most priests experience in one way or another. Halfway through my six years in the priesthood, I fell in love with a woman who was not available. It just happened one day, and I had no control over it. That was it! I had to deal with unrequited love, and the fact that she became a friend made it even more difficult, but somehow, I got through it.

Adventures, Exploits and a Coup D'état

It was always an adventure to drive on African roads. During my first assignment, the roads in the forest were completely rutted by tropical rains and heavy trucks, mostly carrying cocoa or tree trunks. It was not a matter of driving on the right or left, but of driving wherever you could.

On Christmas Day 1978, the drive back to the mission house was slow, noisy, and nerve-wracking. I had driven to a village about twenty miles away to say Mass. My car was a battery-powered Volkswagen Beetle with six volts. On the way back to the mission station, as we were driving up a steep hill, the rear of the car gave off a loud bang. It seemed as if the engine had exploded. I at once switched off the engine. This happened twelve miles from home. The urgency was to get to the mission station in time for Christmas dinner. Under the bonnet, everything was in order; there was no visible damage. So, I started the engine again without any problems, but it made a noise like a tractor. The car moved noisily and was pushed up the steep hill by some locals. The drive back to the station was uneventful but nerve-wracking. It turned out that the problem was just a loose plug caused by the terrible road conditions.

When it comes to those in power, things are certainly managed differently. I remember a trip to Accra to get a new generator for the mission house. I borrowed a flatbed truck for the trip. About twenty miles outside Accra, I was stopped by a police officer who wanted to search the truck. He enquired about the location of the breakdown triangle. There was one somewhere. I looked everywhere but could not find it. *"In that case, I will have to take you to the police station,"* the officer said. I assumed I would have to get into his car or follow him. Instead, he sat down next to me and said, *"Drive."* A few kilometres further on he said, *"You know we can settle this amicably."* *"Oh yes, how?"* I asked. *"All it takes is a few bottles of beer,"* he said. At times, I can be blunt and to the point, so I said, *"I do not believe in giving bribes."* That quietened him, and he said nothing more.

When we arrived in Accra, he made me drive through a maze of streets. I did not know where I was. Finally, he asked me to stop at a petrol station. He got out, closed the door, looked at me through the window and said, *"This time I am just giving you a stern warning."* Then he disappeared. He abandoned me and it was up to me to find out where I was. I would have to find my own way to my destination.

I recall another important incident which happened on 15 May 1979. This was the first time I ever heard the name Jerry Rawlings. My alarm clock rang at 6.00am and as was my habit, I turned on the news. A voice came on the radio and said, "*They have just brought me from my cell. This is Flight Lieutenant Jerry Rawlings. If you have something to fear, you should start running.*" This coup took place at a time of great insecurity in Ghana. Essential commodities were in short supply. Food was scarce; supermarket shelves were almost empty. You had to pay illegal market prices for food or risk travelling to Côte d'Ivoire to get supplies. The currency was devalued at the time, and I remember cocoa farmers taking truckloads of large bags full of money to the bank to exchange it.

Shortly after the coup d'état, the priest in charge went on holiday to Ireland and left it to me to organise the ordination of a local man. This involved a solemn ceremony led by the bishop and a big feast. In a time of such scarcity, where and how was I to get the food for such an event? I heard that someone was selling chickens, but that was an eighty-mile round trip. I was aware that I was taking a risk and could be arrested for transporting fifty or sixty live chickens in my car. I removed the back seat of my VW Beetle and packed all the chickens inside. When I returned to the mission station, the town was swarming with soldiers. They were going from house to house looking for hoarded goods. Thankfully, they were too preoccupied to notice a car loaded with chickens. When we had safely unloaded and stowed the chickens, I felt relieved. Everyone had a wonderful time, and the ordination went smoothly.

Everything about Africa was spectacular, especially the weather. Because of the high humidity, you prayed for rain at the end of the hot season. When the hot season finally ended, the rain came with a thunderous noise. You could hear it approaching as it roared across the forest canopy. I wish I had a rain gauge to measure it. It came down in sheets. The children ran out of their houses and wallowed in the torrential downpour. The lightning that lit up the night sky was magnificent and told me of the majesty and power of the Almighty.

Pastoral Ministry

In Africa, I found a Church that was focused on immediate problems, such as building churches and schools, obtaining cement, and building materials. This was legitimate work and usually fixed the immediate problem, but not the bigger problem the Church was facing. The real problem, in my eyes, was a nominal Church facing a pagan culture.[38]

I remember a confrontation with a tribal chief in one of the villages for which I was responsible. There was a hospital in the main town in the area. Between this town and the village ran a river that was supposed to be home to a 'god.' Women who were menstruating were not allowed to cross the river because they would upset this 'god' as they were considered unclean. In practical terms, they could not cross the river if they had an urgent medical problem that needed to be treated. I asked for a meeting with the chief who was acting on behalf of this 'deity.' The meeting did not go well, and I was politely but unceremoniously shown the door.

African spirituality touches every aspect of human life and people have an incredible hunger for God. I remember a sermon on Pentecost Sunday 1980. I preached on the Baptism in the Holy Spirit and the whole church responded when I asked people to come forward. This surprised me and I did not have the resources to follow up. I realised that there needed to be some fundamental changes in the approach of the Church to develop the culture, the resources or the depth and breadth of leadership to meet that kind of response. That was not going to happen anytime soon.

---

38 A 'nominal' Christian is Christian in name only. Please see Chapter 7 for more information on nominalism.

Finishing My Time in Africa

Towards the end of my time in Africa as a priest, I became quite ill with hepatitis. As I recuperated in hospital, it became clear through God's voice that my time in Ghana was ending. I had a strong feeling that God had a different kind of ministry for me. I was still a priest, but I embarked on a journey to discover what God had in store for me.

During my recovery from hepatitis, I worked in Ireland and visited schools to seek candidates for the priesthood. I was aware of the irony of this, as I was having great doubts about the priesthood myself.

I then learned of a Catholic parish that might be more suited to the style of ministry I was looking for, so with the blessing of my superiors I moved to this new parish.

During my time in Africa, I came to have increasing doubts about the Church. In the following chapter I will outline these doubts and some reasons why I was no longer convinced.

CHAPTER 7

UNCONVINCED

"Don't let the noise of other's opinions drown out
your own inner voice."[39]

Do you ever wrestle with the question, *"Why do I believe what I believe?"* I have, and it began during my years in the seminary. My doubts were never about the existence of God, the reliability of the Bible, or the great biblical teachings of the Church. My doubts centred on extra-biblical teachings and the state of the Church. There were many things of which I was not convinced. One subject that was near the top of the list was nominalism.

Nominalism

It was the night before the battle of Milvian Bridge. The scene was outside Rome, and it was the year AD 312. The Roman Emperor Constantine was preparing for battle the next day. He prayed for success. He either had a vision or a dream. Constantine saw a picture with the inscription *"in hoc signo vinces"* (*"in this sign, conquer"*). There is some debate about what sign he saw. Some say he saw a cross. Others say he saw the letters *Chi* and *Rho*,

---

39 Steve Jobs

the first two Greek letters of the word Christ. Whatever Constantine saw or experienced, he attributed his victory the following day to the Christian God. The outcome of this vision was dramatic for the Christian Church. *"Almost overnight, it was the 'done thing' to be a Christian; and to be a Christian minister was to have honour and prestige. Thousands joined the Church and many – without any sense of divine calling or vocation – became 'clergy.'"*[40] Those who were received into the Church were not instructed in the true principles of Christianity. This event at Milvian Bridge laid the foundation for what is known as 'nominal Christianity.' The result was that a persecuted, fit for purpose Church grew *"fat and comfortable"* allowing toxic trends to take hold.

Before this development in the Church, in the first three hundred years of Church history, priests and bishops lived a peaceful married life until they were invaded by misogynists, control freaks and ascetics. Priests were then herded through Institutionalised terrorism into the enclosure of celibacy against their will. This was a toxic trend resulting from the 'paganisation' of Christianity.

Nominalism has to do with empty rituals and meaningless formalities. A nominal Christian is a Christian in name only, who may have grown up repeating the catechism without having any experience of the gospel or the power of the Holy Spirit. There are people who call themselves Christians even though they have never set foot in a church. Others attend church, but it is only a formality. Christ has no influence on their lives and people have no concept of having a personal relationship with Him. They do not read the Bible, witness to others, or take nourishment from attending church. For a

---

40 David Allen, *The Unfailing Stream: A Charismatic Church History in* Outline (Tonbridge, Sovereign World, 1994), p.25

nominal Christian, religion is not something that requires a change of heart or lifestyle. It does not require anything in terms of morality or responsibility. George Bernard Shaw summed up the concept of nominalism when he said that *"Christianity never got a grip of the world until it virtually reduced its claims on the ordinary citizen's attention to every seventh day and let him alone on a week-days."*[41]

Culture

In addition to nominalism, listening to my inner voice led to a sense of foreboding about being in the right Church. I did not seem to fit the culture. This unsettling, unrelenting feeling of being in the wrong place churned in the pit of my stomach. Perhaps you have experienced this uneasy feeling too. It hurts so much that it feels like physical pain.

In 1979 I returned from Africa with an Ashanti stool. It is a beautiful unique piece of carving. But we have difficulty finding out where it belongs in our house. Occasionally we use it as a seat, but the question is where does it belong? It is visually appealing and sometimes used, but it does not seem to fit in with our general décor and aesthetic design. We could change everything in our home to match the stool, but then our home would no longer reflect who we are. The solution is to hide it in a corner where it will not be noticed.

I cannot say that I was ever entirely comfortable in the role of priest. I was an 'Ashanti stool.' My evolving beliefs did not seem to fit in anywhere, and there were many aspects of the whole experience that made me uncomfort-

---

41 Ned Sherrin, *The Oxford Dictionary of Humorous Quotations* (Oxford, Oxford University Press, 1995), p.270

able. It was strange to have people address me as 'Father.' I felt more comfortable without the Roman collar than with it. I was very unhappy with the concept of accepting gifts of money in return for saying Mass. The pressure to conform to the established system was immense. From the beginning, I swam against the tide. I struggled with the culture.

What exactly is culture? Simply put, culture can be defined as "*the way things are done around here.*" Changing the culture of the Church is as difficult as nailing jelly to a tree. One of the reasons for this is that we are only aware of a tiny part of it. It is like an iceberg. The culture of the Catholic Church has developed over almost two thousand years and is deeply rooted in the community. Someone once said, "*The Church thinks in centuries.*" I was not going to change that. It would take much more than the views of a single dissenting priest to bring about change.

You cannot blame the people for the problems of the Church. There is a deeper, systemic problem, and the culture must change. The culture rewards conformity, uncritical loyalty to Rome and a safe pair of hands, rather than integrity, faithfulness to scripture, passion for Christ and creativity in proclaiming the gospel. It excludes many gifted and capable men and women who are called to both marriage and the priesthood. The system prevents ordinary Catholics from having a say in the overall governance of the Church.

I realised that I did not belong. I had to find a church culture into which I could fit. I did not fit into the absolutist and intransigent Roman system that was uncoordinated with what the Holy Spirit was saying. I did not want to spend the rest of my life as an 'Ashanti stool' swimming against the tide and feeling like I was going nowhere fast. As I got older, I realised that you must fit in and flow with the culture, not the other way around. "*When you are in Rome, do what the Romans do,*" and if you feel you cannot go with the

Romans, then leave Rome. I concluded that I had to do just that. I should have done it much earlier.

Doctrine

I became unconvinced about the doctrines of the Church, especially the teaching on salvation. I had been seeking salvation on the back of works or charitable deeds. *"Be good, for God is watching you,"* our parents, priests and teachers told us as children. As Brennan Manning puts it, *"The bending of the mind by the powers of this world had twisted the gospel of grace into religious bondage and distorted the image of God into an eternal, small-minded book-keeper."*[42] In modern dialect, God had a spreadsheet and he kept account of everything. On one column He recorded all your bad deeds and on a parallel column He recorded your good ones. However, your good deeds never counterbalanced your evil ones. Consequently, I was constantly chasing brownie points and trying to endear myself to God by being 'good.'

A doctrine that had been hidden in the attic of the Church for fifteen hundred years was retrieved and dusted off by Martin Luther and the reformers. It had been hidden in an old Bible in our house for the first fifteen years of my life. In my teenage years, I dusted it off and found some of the Bible's hidden gems. My discovery over the following years was astounding. We have been restored to a right relationship with God and it is not by our own merits. We owe it solely to His mercy, granted to us through the life,

---

42 Brennan Manning, *The Ragamuffin Gospel, Embracing the Unconditional Love of God* (London, Authentic Media, 2001), p.1

death, and resurrection of His Son Jesus Christ. The Good News is the gospel of God's gift of salvation to us.

I had been staggering around like a blind man trying to get right with God. It only took a couple of verses from the Bible to convince me, and my eyes were opened. These verses from the book of Ephesians said, *"For it is by grace you have been saved, through faith—and this is not from yourselves, it is the gift of God— not by works, so that no one can boast. For we are God's handiwork, created in Christ Jesus to do good works, which God prepared in advance for us to do."*[43] I compare it to a race where you put all your effort into crossing the finish line. Then suddenly you realise that you have already broken the tape. In fact, you crossed the finish line before you started. You are already home. Salvation is not about what I **do**, or what the Church does for me. Salvation is about what the Lord has **done**. I put my faith in Jesus alone for my salvation.

If you have come to believe in salvation as a gift of God's grace, you will next ask yourself, *"But what about good works?"* Does not the Epistle of James say that faith is dead unless it is accompanied by works?[44] I had to try to make sense of this. There are many answers, but I settled on one that seems most obvious and makes the most sense to me.

Intellectual 'faith' does not require action or response. Many 'religious' people excel in intellectual faith. However, this kind of faith does not lead to transformation. Saving faith which comes from your heart, on the other hand, is dynamic and life changing. In other words, we are saved only by faith, but this saving faith will produce good works in us. Faith that has moved from the mind to the heart is transformative. This saving faith writes God's law of

---

43 Ephesians 2:8-10
44 James 2:17

love on your heart.[45] The law is no longer written on tablets of stone or pages in a book. It is engraved deep inside you. When you truly accept the price that has been paid for you, love will naturally flow from your heart. If I say I believe in Christ but just continue my old life, I have no real saving faith and cannot say I am saved. If I have not changed, my faith is "*dead.*"

Relying on works alone was very uncomfortable. In my daily living, I tried to be as good as possible, but this gave me little confidence. One day you feel loved and the next unlovable. I was on a perfectionist roller coaster ride. When I discovered 'grace', I found that God's love is not based on my performance and that he loves me even when I am unlovable. The truth is that nothing we do can make God love us more or be more pleased with our human achievement. We find favour in God's eyes, not through the good works we try to do, but simply because He loves us so much that he sent Jesus as the sacrifice that takes away our sins.

I went on to discover that the Bible does not mention purgatory, infant Baptism, Marian devotion, compulsory priestly celibacy, or papal infallibility. I found it hard to believe that the bread and wine were changed into the literal body and blood of Christ. It is clear from the Bible that a Christian should never pray to a saint because Jesus Christ is the only one who can speak to the Almighty on our behalf.[46] The doctrine of salvation that emphasised works and not grace was not a biblical doctrine. Furthermore, I was unconvinced about the Church because it had lost the power of Pentecost and seemed content to encourage a nominal brand of Christianity.

---

45 Ezekiel 36:26
46 1 Timothy 2:5

Lack of Power

I discovered a power vacuum in the Church, and by that I do not mean that the higher ups lacked authority. The Church lacked the power of the Holy Spirit. After my encounter with God, I wanted to find out more about the Holy Spirit. I knew that He is the third Person of the Trinity, but there was little emphasis on His work in the Church. I knew from the Creed that He is *"the Lord, the giver of life,"* but that was it. I wanted to find out more.

I was baptised as a baby and confirmed at the age of eleven. I remember the day of my Confirmation very clearly. I do not remember much about the ceremony, but I remember the time afterwards; it bucketed it down or as we say, *"It rained cats and dogs."*[47] That day, when I was eleven, we experienced ridiculously heavy rain. For me, it was a prophetic sign of what the Spirit would do in my life later. I experienced the Baptism in the Holy Spirit as a drenching, pouring over, and soaking through. The heavens opened and it seemed as if all the heavenly rain that was possible that day fell on me. There was a significant difference between the day of my Confirmation and the day of my Baptism in the Holy Spirit.

This experience led me to accept that Confirmation should be more than the bishop laying hands on your head and nothing happening. As I talked to people and studied Pentecostal doctrine, I discovered that for Pentecostals, the Baptism in the Holy Spirit (or Confirmation) is an actual experience that equips a person with power to serve God. Something happens. It is an experience distinct from and following conversion that gives the Christian power to serve. There is a time delay. This is called the doctrine of 'subsequence.' In

---

47 Cats and dogs used to sleep on the roofs of thatched houses and slide or slip down when it started to rain.

other words, it is an experience that is different from receiving the Holy Spirit at conversion and occurs later. I began to believe that this experience applies to all Christians, not just a select few. It is a clear, distinct experience in a person's life that leaves no doubt that something extraordinary has happened.

Baptism in the Holy Spirit is accompanied by speaking in tongues. About three weeks after my remarkable experience in the seminary, I was invited to a Catholic Charismatic prayer meeting. The aim of these meetings was to renew the Church through the power of the Holy Spirit. It was at this meeting that I spoke in tongues for the first time.

Although these experiences are documented in the New Testament, they disappeared from the Church for centuries, except for occasional occurrences. Where they did occur, it was because thirsty souls cried out for living water. God met their need irrespective of gender, race, colour, or any other circumstance. Thirst was the criteria.

Then on 18 April 1906, the Los Angeles Times sensationally reported the birth of what became known as the Pentecostal movement.[48] This new movement brought with it a strange practice that was to become an unusual doctrine – speaking in tongues as the 'initial evidence' that one had been baptised in the Holy Spirit. This doctrine is a distinguishing feature of most Pentecostal denominations – especially the largest, the Assemblies of God. The Assemblies of God have since dropped the word 'initial' and replaced it with the less controversial words 'biblical evidence.'

This auspicious encounter with God had a startling effect on me. It left me unconvinced concerning the rituals and the way the sacraments of the Church were conducted. Were they just empty formalities that distracted

---

48 James R. Goff, *Charles Parham's Endtime Revival: The Eschatological Expectations of Tongue Speech in Early Pentecostalism.* (Springfield, Missouri, The Flower Pentecostal Heritage Centre Archives), p.87

from the reality and immensity of faith? Were they manufactured and arbitrary and used by the Church to control, influence, and exploit people? I now accept that rituals can be okay if they are based on the teaching of Jesus, and we do not use them to keep people under control or try to put boundaries around the power of the Spirit. We need to be aware of their limitations and understand that they are only essential as far as they are biblically based, and that grace is only released in response to faith and not in an automated manner.

Clericalism

One of the dangers Pope Francis regularly speaks out against is clericalism, and rightly so. But what is he saying? He denounces the clerical culture in which abuse has found a home but does nothing to remove it. Clericalism continues to create an arrogant, controlling spirit of entitlement in the ranks of the priesthood. Among the laity it leads to a lazy attitude to service and a false subordination to the clergy.

I was not convinced by the idea that there is an order of importance within the believing community. Uta Ranke-Heinemann maintains that the Council of Trent, in decreeing that celibacy has a higher value than marriage, had in mind their own higher value, "*which they wanted to establish by a doctrinal principle*."[49] I could not accept that those lower down in the ranks were seen as inferior. I was becoming more convinced that all believers are "*kings and priests*" and a "*holy priesthood*."[50] This is because we are heirs of the Kingdom

---

49 Uta Ranke-Heinemann, *Eunuchs for the Kingdom of Heaven*, p.114
50 1 Peter 2:9

of God. We have access to His seat of power through Jesus Christ. We are all priests and have the same status. Everyone has direct access to God's grace, which does not have to be mediated to us through other means. There is no difference between clergy and laity and no special reverence should be given, apart from the respect that should be given to someone in an official position.

As I witnessed lay Catholics using the gifts of the Holy Spirit to bless and encourage the Church, I concluded that all should be freed from clerical control. On one occasion I was part of a group that witnessed a gifted woman guide us in casting out a demon of infirmity. The sick woman was bedridden, could not move and had crippling pain in her back. The woman who led us had a vision of a demon slamming its claws into the woman's back. We were encouraged to pray. The pain moved from her back to her knee. We continued to pray and eventually the pain moved down her leg and out the soles of her feet. The sick woman got out of bed and ran through the house shouting praises to God.

The role that enthusiastic and gifted women can play in ministry should not be restricted. Those in the pews must have a future in ministry and be guided by the inspiration of the Holy Spirit. The sad reality is that many gifted Christians have to endure an endless series of formal events and ceremonies led by clergy, dressed in strange clothing, often communicating in a strange, ethereal or sometimes monotonous tone. Gifted people have become passive spectators attending a live performance.

I came to believe that there is no inherent change that takes place in a person when he is called to an office in the Church. In early Christianity there is only an egalitarian movement. This 'caste system' of clericalism is a legacy of the Roman Empire.

I could find no reference in the New Testament to such a hierarchy within the believing community. The apostles appointed by Jesus were never given the title of priest. There is no indication in the New Testament that the apostles established a priesthood as God had established through Moses in the Old Testament. The New Testament ministry was about servant leadership and the use of gifts to bring people to maturity in Christ, not about offering sacrifices.[51]

Rituals

During my time as a priest, I became disillusioned with the constant parade of elaborate rituals and the outward display of religious devotion. There is nothing wrong with the outward display of reverence unless it presents itself as nominalism clothed in elaborate rituals. I saw that rituals were performed because they had always been done that way. There was no room for creativity or for the work of the Holy Spirit. This aroused in me a deep distrust towards these practices. Because the Church functions according to a pre-programmed system, the way the services are conducted does not convey a sense of God's presence, let alone a personal God. In short, the sense of closeness to God the Father is not there.

How did it come about that the Church began to suppress the presence of God? A crucial point in the history of the Church came when all the witnesses of the New Testament Church had died. Certain harmful ideas and practices began to creep into the Church. These ideas were not found in the Bible. As the Church moved away from the teachings of the Bible, it was very damaging to the Church.

---

51 Ephesians 4:11-13

One of the innovative ideas was called 'sacraments.' Sacraments are an outward sign of an unseen spiritual reality in which God is believed to share his grace with a person. The word sacrament is not found in the Bible, but the concept is. The two sacraments that Jesus left us are Baptism and Communion (Breaking of Bread). The Church instituted five additional sacraments not found in the Bible. It began to teach that 'grace' comes only through the official ministry of the Church in an almost automated manner, through the sacraments administered by the clergy. This gave the clergy a privileged role and paved the way for the introduction of clericalism and priesthood. It also marginalised ordinary gifted Christians whose spiritual gifts were now redundant.

While most people around me were excited by the sacraments and externals of Catholicism, I was more interested in experiencing the presence of God and the power of the Holy Spirit, and in communicating the presence of God to His people. At the same time, I was looking for a context within Catholicism where I could see a move away from automation and nominalism towards a genuine, authentic New Testament Christianity.

Celibacy and Loneliness

Loneliness hit me hard during my time in Africa. I felt quite isolated, not only because of celibacy, but also because of the enormity of the task and my doubts and reservations about the Church. This loneliness was a constant pain that nothing could heal. I felt a deep and inescapable sense of isolation. I could not talk to anyone about it because I was not supposed to feel that way. I was a celibate priest who had given up his home and family, and should not Christ be enough for me? Vatican II had encouraged me that God's grace would be enough. Celibacy, I was told, was a gift from God that priests should seek through prayer. According to the Church, it is possible for any priest to be celibate if he seeks the grace of God.

While I avoided opportunities to become overly familiar with the opposite sex, I did miss having a life partner, and I was surprised at how intense the loneliness was. Maybe I was not praying hard enough!

I got up every morning at 6.00am to find an empty house. The day consisted of a variety of tasks until I went for siesta at 1.00pm. At 4.00pm, after showering and getting ready, I set off to visit an outstation. On each visit, you visited the homes of all the Catholics, heard their confessions and held a service. This was my routine – moving from outstation to outstation in the forest, sleeping on a small camp bed with a lamp powered by my car battery. The nights were the worst times as you sat alone, with only the mosquitoes or a bat flying over your head to keep you company. There was no television, computers, or smartphones to distract you. I felt lonely and when I could find it, I started drinking alcohol to cope with the dark thoughts that haunted me. I never got 'fluthered'[52] but on occasion I knew I had crossed a line. That screamed failure because my spiritual life was supposed to support all my needs.

In Africa, I appreciated the communal life I occasionally shared with my fellow priests, but I also felt the debilitating loneliness that resulted from a life that lacked the deep personal intimacy that married couples enjoy. There was a disconnect between the relationships I had and the relationships I wanted. Thoughts about marriage resurfaced and I began to waver about celibacy.

---

52 Means blind drunk, intoxicated. Originally a Dublin word but it spread throughout the country and now is featured in the global dictionary.

My own batteries were running down, and my ministry was beginning to run on empty. It was not a life. I was only serving a system, and if I had been willing to continue to compromise, or if I had been content to fulfil the formalities of religion for the rest of my life in a state of *"existential solitude,"* I would have ended up in deep despair. This was the culmination of a life of clericalism, self-denial, and celibacy, a life in the service of a pre-programmed system.

The thought of giving up the priesthood sometimes crossed my mind. The pain and discomfort of living without vision, without a sense of mission and with false teachings became too much to bear. Following the rigid routines of Catholicism for the rest of my life was unimaginable. Africa was an exciting place, but the old rigid and repetitive routines of Catholicism bored me. I had to find a way out.

As a seminarian I had been happy, surrounded by friends and an incredibly supportive environment. The missionary society that recruited me had put a lot of thought into creating a friendly and caring way of life for its students. You never thought too much about what life would be like in pastoral ministry after ordination. Dr Bartemeier, a leading psychiatrist once said: *"We take promising young men from thirteen to twenty-five years of age, feed them well, educate them diligently, and eight to twelve years later we ordain them, healthy, bright, emotional thirteen-year-olds."*[53]

From my youth I taught myself to spiritualise my sexuality. In my mind, I had desexualised love, just like Saint Augustine, even though I knew nothing about him. I found, however, that it is part of being human to have impulses and urges that cannot be directed or prayed away. That is the thing about

---

53 A.W. Richard Sipe, *Celibacy in Crisis: A Secret World Revisited* (Kindle edition: Brunner-Routledge, 2003), Location 529

human impulses, they are instinctive desires that you can never get rid of. At first, you might knowingly suffocate these thoughts, but over time, they always resurface, stronger than ever. Controlling them is the great struggle of the celibate priest.

If you do not have the gift of celibacy, you will find the solution in the Bible. It is called marriage. St Paul confronted me with this truth from the Bible when he said, *"Now to the unmarried and the widows I say: It is good for them to stay unmarried, as I do. But if they cannot control themselves, they should marry, for it is better to marry than to burn with passion."* [54] There is great wisdom in the Word of God, for if a priest cannot find a way out in marriage, he will find other means of release, most of which are unhealthy and sinful. A priest should be able to make things right by entering into a lawful marriage without abandoning his ministry.

I could no longer pretend that human sexuality did not apply to me. I was still a man. Since the 1960s, we have lived in a highly sexualised world. Sex is everywhere and there is no escaping it. A.W. Richard Sipe rightly pointed out that, *"Priests striving for celibacy live, move, and have their being in a distinctly sexually aware and sexually active world."* [55] My world was about to be shaken and challenged when I stepped out of my sheltered ivory tower into a sexually explicit world, albeit a world thinly veiled by charismatic spirituality.

During my time as a priest, I was linked to the Catholic Charismatic movement. Charismatic prayer meetings are gatherings of Christians who come together to thank, praise, and worship God under the guidance of the Holy Spirit. The nature of the meetings fostered relationships and friendships. I had always sacrificed my deep longing for love and companionship

---

54 1 Corinthians 7:9

55 A.W. Richard Sipe, *Celibacy in Crisis* (Kindle Edition), Location 424

to engage in ministry. But my life of prayer and self-discipline could not turn off hormones. In the immediate physical proximity of these charismatic encounters, I became increasingly aware of my humanity. For a priest who had been trained to lead a solitary life without close contact with people, I had now entered dangerous territory.

Having strictly followed the Church rule of celibacy, I had never dated a woman. I knew the church rules about touching and looking, which applied to single people and engaged couples. All were warned against 'sins of immodesty.' If this was already required of 'normal' Catholics, how much more of celibate priests?

The first time a girl hugged me at a charismatic meeting, I was completely taken aback. It touched me so much that I still remember it. I was not used to physical affection. At these charismatic meetings there were many opportunities to get closer. I had a few close friendships but leaving the priesthood was not something I wanted or was ready to do. Sometimes, during open confession, there was electricity in the air as the lady held my hands and unburdened herself to me. Our eyes could so easily have met, and we could have been taken in by the moment. Thankfully, apart from hugging, nothing happened in any of these relationships.

As time passed, I was already mentally on my way out and open to a relationship. I had surrendered full control of my life to an institution that expected me to perform my ministry in an almost mechanised way. When Jesus went away into heaven and the Holy Spirit came, He brought with him a whole lot of conviction.[56] I was convicted that I was not in the right place. As a result, I now wanted to go beyond the boundaries I had accepted as a priest of the Latin rite. It would be difficult and uncertain. Although I did not

56 John 16:8

know it at the time, I was still an emotional adolescent, and I was entering unknown territory.

I was also influenced by some of the views of the time about having normal, social friendships with women, even a close relationship. A clinical psychologist named Desmond O'Donnell wrote in the Furrow in 1972: "*Every priest needs normal contact with women as a source of personal and apostolic enrichment. The priest's normal social and apostolic contacts with women may lead him to a closer relationship with one or several. This can be very valuable for him, provided he has reached a degree of faith and maturity to sustain it.*"[57]

We were encouraged that this experience of love could be beneficial and add a new dimension to our personality. My "*normal social and apostolic contact*" led me to a closer relationship. It was the first time I ventured into this world in which I allowed my vulnerability and desire for companionship to come out. This 'secret' relationship did not last. We were not right for each other. I was very immature and had a lot of growing up to do.

Paul Scanlon says: "*Separation is the first act of possession. If you want to receive something, then you must let go of something first. It is a life-principle.*"[58] I wanted to marry, but my mistake was to seek a relationship before I resolved my relationship with the priesthood. This led to inner conflict and confusion. When you enter a relationship as a celibate priest, you are wading into the murky waters of clandestine relationships, and you are constantly looking over your shoulder. When you hide a relationship from others, you feel shame. Celibacy was the official line, but for many who struggled with it, 'clandestine' was the unofficial way. In the future, I would not go down that path. It was not fair to anyone.

---

57 Desmond O'Donnell, *Celibacy* (Maynooth, The Furrow, February 1972), p.82
58 Paul Scanlon, *Crossing Over* (Tonbridge, Sovereign World, 2002), p.12

Today I know that I should not have taken the secret path. From this I learned that one should not enter into any new agreements, relationships, or contracts until one has resolved the existing ones. I do not have a spotless record in this matter. But what I do have is experience. I have often used this experience to counsel anyone in marriage break up. *"Do not enter into another relationship until you have resolved your existing one,"* is always my advice.

After five years in the priesthood, the tensions in my life were increasing and I was very restless. However, it was an abusive encounter with a senior member of the clergy that did me great harm and brought my misgivings and restlessness to the moment of resolution. I was heartbroken and had no idea how I would ever muster the strength to regain my freedom. But I simply closed my eyes and took a leap of faith. Overcoming the consequences of an abusive encounter requires conscious decisions and positive steps every day to bring one's life back into balance.

CHAPTER 8

SPIRITUAL ABUSE

"While they curse, may you bless."[59]

It is shocking to learn that spiritual abuse is alive in the Church. Sexual abuse is well documented, but we seldom hear about spiritual abuse. However, the issue that moved me towards the door more quickly than anything else was a painful experience of spiritual abuse. That was the tipping point. It made me so dysfunctional that I could no longer live with the situation. I already had many reasons to quit, but this focused me on the end game more than anything else.

The background to this encounter was my move to a parish in the UK after returning from Africa.

I was still figuring out how God's call would play out in my life as I continued to work in this new parish. I was still seeking a setting within the church where I felt comfortable to serve as a priest. But then something happened that forced my hand. It tipped the balance.

If someone who has spiritual authority over you uses their position to manipulate, control or dominate you, causing you spiritual harm, this is by definition spiritual abuse. However, this does not always happen from the top down. Anyone in a position of trust can coerce and control others. Many

---

59 Psalm 109:28

who have been abused themselves become abusers in turn. Someone who claims to have instructions from God can manipulate others because they are assumed to stand for God. I was certainly subjected to *"coercive controlling behaviour."* Lundy Bancroft, author, and consultant on abuse, is quoted as saying, *"Abuse grows from attitudes and values, not feelings. The roots are ownership, the trunk is entitlement, and the branches are control."*[60]

The immediate reason for this encounter with the senior churchman from the diocese was a misjudgement on my part. I will not go into details to protect identities, but I had made a mistake. Nothing illegal or immoral happened. My contract in the parish was expiring and I was informed that it would not be renewed. This was hurtful and I left the Parish centre and ended up in local accommodation that was too close for his liking. At that point, no alternative arrangements had been found for me.

Nothing could have prepared me for what awaited me that evening when we had this encounter. There were no formalities, and the meeting was short. He was calm and focused; he said what he wanted to say without giving me a chance to respond. In any case, his source of authority was ownership and he made it clear to me that I had no business on his turf. I do not remember his exact words, but everything about him showed a certain sense of entitlement. It showed in the way he wiped the floor with me. Someone else might have 'decked' him, but I was so caught off guard that I did not see it coming. It was a knockout punch. A conversation or discussion about his reasons could have softened the blow. When a good football manager wants to move a player on from the club, he has a conversation with him and does so in a respectful

---

60 Lundy Bancroft, *Why Does He Do That? Inside the Minds of Angry and Controlling Men*, https://www.goodreads.com/quotes/tag/controlling-people

manner. But here there was no conversation and certainly no respect, just a monologue to put me in my place and unmistakably exert control.

The Message Bible says, "*Words kill, words give life; they are either poison or fruit – the choice is yours.*"[61] The book of Proverbs also reminds us, "*The words of the reckless pierce like swords, but the tongue of the wise brings healing.*"[62] The immediate effect on me was shocking. Was this God's judgement on me coming from a man of the cloth whom I respected and had come to know well? This pronouncement by God's messenger was like a lightning bolt from a cloudless sky that aimed to make me pay for questioning the Church.

Chernobyl

I have racked my brains for years wondering if such a thing is normal. From that moment on, my life practically fell apart. Everything changed that night, and my life has never been the same since. It was a Chernobyl-like experience. Eric Maddison, my mentor, wrote, "*Sweeping through our society at hurricane strength is a twentieth-century tornado called rejection. Lives are being lost, homes destroyed, and families torn apart as it gathers increasing momentum. The damage done by this Satan-inspired scourge is deep within the personality, striking at the roots of an individual's personhood.*"[63]

This hurricane force phenomenon tore through my life and the immediate internal damage was devastating. Externally, the fallout contaminated everything, and the effects lasted for years. It infected my mind to such an

---

61 Proverbs 18:21-23

62 Proverbs 12:18

63 Eric Maddison, *Are You Missing God's Best*? (Chichester, New Wine Press, 2004), p.59

extent that big picture thinking went out the window. It lowered my self-esteem and dignity, and the harsh voices of judgement and confusion had a field day in my mind.

While I never rejected or cursed God, in my brokenness and dejection I drifted further and further into realms of sorrow and self-hatred. In coming to the UK, I had stepped out and made myself vulnerable and I was now engulfed in the black hole of grief. As St Augustine said about his time of barrenness and sorrow, "*I sank away from Thee, and I wandered, O my God, too much astray from Thee my stay, in these days of my youth, and I became to myself a barren land.*"[64]

Fallout

I describe the year after this incident as my 'annus horribilis' in which my life went off the rails. I lost the ability to have healthy relationships and I hurt people who meant a lot to me. I became insensitive and incapable of real feelings. Consequently, I treated some people badly. It is true that hurt people hurt other people and even the gentlest soul can be held hostage to unkind behaviour and behave in the most unloving of ways following abuse.

I had difficulty reading situations and made some bad decisions. My life was an unmitigated "khazi,"[65] an unspeakable disaster for a perfectionist cleric who aspired to an ascetic lifestyle. During my ministry duties, I felt empty and powerless because I had nothing to offer. Not knowing what to do, how

---

64 Saint Augustine, *The Confessions of Saint Augustine* (Translated by E.B. Pusey, Kindle book), Book (II) Location 458

65 A khazi is a slang word for a toilet, used in Liverpool and parts of London.

to cope or how to recover, my life became a kamikaze mission. I became a pilot on a hopeless mission, crashing his plane into a target and getting hurt in the event.

My feelings were raw and intense. The actor, Clint Eastwood once said, *"Respect your efforts, respect yourself. Self-respect leads to self-discipline. When you have both firmly under your belt, that's real power."*[66]

Self-esteem and self-discipline were ripped from me, and with them *"real power."* It happened overnight. I did not recognise the person I had become. I had no desire to live on the wild side, but I did things that were out of character. It felt like I was outside the world I once belonged to, and it made no sense.

Why?

There had to be an explanation for the way I responded in such a messed-up manner. To quote Eric Maddison again: *"Rejection damage is one of the main reasons for a rebellious attitude toward any authority figure, such as parents, police, and even God."*[67] My 'backsliding' only magnified and intensified the original pain of the abuse. It brought much more confusion and shame into my life. I had been an advocate for people putting their lives together and my life was falling apart. That was shameful.

There was a second realisation that helped my rational mind understand the mess I was in. I experienced what I can only describe as a kind of excommunication when I was asked to leave the parish to which I belonged. I was

66 Clint Eastwood, https://www.brainyquote.com/quotes/clint_eastwood_392797
67 Eric Maddison, *Are You Missing God's Best?* p.59

unofficially excluded from that community and from the group of Christians I was with. We can agree that fellowship helps us grow spiritually and connects us with other believers. The term 'Bible fellowship' describes the mutual support, encouragement, and accountability that believers enjoy in the community.

Without fellowship, a Christian is in danger of being attacked by seducing evil spirits. As I found out later, involvement in a good local church increases your desire for personal holiness and Christlikeness. When you live under the security of godly leadership and sound biblical teaching, you will quickly recognise deception and more easily resist the temptation to fall away from the Lord. Other believers will also encourage you to live for the glory of God.

Thirdly, I had lost sight of my true nature through the pain of rejection. If we live in the power of our new nature, we walk in fellowship with God.[68] However, as soon as we lose sight of who we are in Christ we begin to act against our true God-given nature. I now had to refocus my gaze on Jesus and allow my new nature to control my behaviour so that I could consistently live a godly life again.

This incident also caused me to take a closer look at my perfectionist approach to life. I went into a downward spiral of self-reproach and guilt. You know you have a strong tendency towards perfectionism when you keep telling yourself, "*I should not have messed up! I am a failure. I should be a better person. At my age, I should have known bette*r!" I had an obsessive focus and always wanted to be better. D.S. Burns would say that I had written myself a script for self-defeat when he wrote: "*Perfectionist individuals, we find, are likely to respond to the perception of failure or inadequacy with a*

---

68 1 John 3:9b

precipitous loss in self-esteem that can trigger episodes of severe depression and anxiety.[69]

Overcoming this quest for perfection was one of the greatest struggles in my life. Not being good enough was the birth chamber for massive feelings of guilt and shame. Because of my perfectionism, I was vulnerable to rejection, but my outward appearance betrayed that to no one. That senior churchman had no idea what was going on inside me and I do not blame him for what happened. If I play the blame game, I am giving power to the man who hurt me. If I met him today, I would shake his hand. As for the others who have hurt me, they owe me nothing. Nor do I blame my upbringing or the people who influenced my life. There is no point in getting angry with people who mislead, betray or hurt you. You just bow gracefully out of their lives, enjoy the new journey, and welcome the new friends and allies you make along the way.

God's Plan

It is not possible to deal with an ambush if you do not have the necessary means. In this situation, why were my resilience and emotional resources so lacking? It was a bridge too far. It must also be said that if the means had been available to deal with this sad situation, I would have kept putting off the decision to leave the Church. But God, in His mercy, led me into the valley of decision. We can be very quick to say, *"God did not do that,"* but who can say that God did not bring me down so that He could raise me up? He brought

---

69 David S Burns, *The Perfectionist's Script for self-Defeat* (Psychology Today, N.Y.), p.34

me down so that He could deal with me, but also to prepare me for the task ahead. He wanted me to be fit for purpose.

Even though life was a complete failure, God was present in all the pain and suffering. He was already preparing me for another mission field. He had already lined up the events, the relationships, and the calling that I had no idea about at that time.

When is the right time?

The consequences of my personal 'Chernobyl' continued to occupy me for a long time. I have many reasons to talk about an event that profoundly changed my life, but anger and resentment are not among them. Putting my memories down on paper was very therapeutic because it helped me gain new insights and come to terms with my experiences and choices.

How do I know that this is the right time to tell what happened to me? For one thing, a lot of time has passed, and a lot of water has flowed under the bridge. Time does not heal all wounds; what helps is to actively work on your healing and not to get stuck. I have stopped asking 'why?' because I have realised that God had a plan for me all along.

One indicator that you are ready to tell your story is when you realise that the whole rejection thing was not about you. It was all about their problems, insecurity, and fear. Yes, I made mistakes, and I had my own issues, but in the end, I was not the problem. To show some empathy, I had to see beyond the clerical collar and the stark authority bestowed on the priest by a powerful Church. I did not know the story of the human being who hurt me, but it did help to realise that there had to be a reason for his behaviour. Hurt people hurt people. Heal yourself by having some compassion for them.

Exiting

While it had seemed the right thing to do, to work for a renewal of the Catholic Church, I now knew the only way left was to resign. This was the end of the line; it really was over for me. I had stayed so long because I could inwardly protest the system and its teachings. Leaving would cause great pain to those I cared about. Deborah Layton, a Jonestown survivor, wrote: "*We are in a cult when we consider staying in a group because we cannot bear the loss, disappointment and grief our leaving will cause ourselves and those we have come to love.*"[70]

The importance that the Catholic Church had was now gone. Confusion was the order of the day in many ways, but one thing was certain – it was time for me to leave. There was no doubt that this was the right path. But at the same time there was a sense of disappointment. The original plan was to achieve something, to remain a priest for life and to respond to what seemed at the time like God's guidance. The depth of disappointment was in direct proportion to the amount of investment made over the years. The more you commit, the more disappointed you are when it does not work out. But now the whole situation was extremely damaging to my personal well-being. Walking away from my faith in Jesus was never on the cards. I owed my allegiance to Him. I would not abandon the body of Christ, but I left the Church in which I grew up. The fact is that I could no longer trust the clergy.

I was resigned that I was in a Church that could offer me no rehabilitation. I had tried my best and sought a healthy context for ministry, but it was a complete failure. Nowhere could I find the support I needed and was looking

---

70 Deborah Layton, *Seductive Poison: A Jonestown Survivor's Story of Life and Death in the Peoples Temple* (Palatine, Anchor Books, 1999), p.299

for. This is not to belittle the efforts of many wonderful people and the work of my own missionary society who tried to help.

"*I wish it need not have happened in my time,*" said Frodo. '*So do I,*' said Gandalf, '*and so do all who live to see such times. But that is not for them to decide. All we must decide is what to do with the time that is given us.*"[71]

As soon as I was strong enough, I had to decide what to do with the time I had been given. I could continue to indulge my self-hatred, or I could explore the possibility of reshaping my life. When one falls into this state of self-hatred, it is difficult to find the courage to rebuild what has been lost. Rebuilding can be a slow process. It is possible to regain self-respect, but it takes the grace of God and a lot of effort and determination. Rejection and failure can be a big blow and often stops you from trying again. However, I was determined not to waste my life but to make the most of it.

This fateful encounter with the priest was the turning point. Ironically, it proved to be a blessing. God turned the heat up so much that I had to get out. It became too uncomfortable to continue. It is amazing that the things that cause us the most pain are often the ones we look back on with the most gratitude. That gave me the incentive to do what I should have done a long time ago.

It was a big mistake to join. All I can do is raise my hands and say, "*It was my mistake. I take responsibility.*" My life choices had an impact on many people and there was no way to make amends. With better information, I might have made a different decision and had a better outcome. But the situation had given me a unique opportunity. I had to decide to move on and I had to stand up and say, "*I do not care how hard this is, I do not care how*

---

71 J.R.R. Tolkien, *Lord of The Rings Trilogy, The Fellowship of the Rings* (London, HarperCollins, 1995), Book 1, Chapter 2, p.50

devastated I am. This thing is not going to overwhelm me. People will be hurt, but I am going to obey God." If you want your life to count, you must count the cost. It has often been said that *"our greatest challenges are our greatest opportunities."*

After that, my entire world would change. *"Your rejection is your new direction,"* Paul Scanlon once preached. That rejection and pain was the beginning of God's plan for my life. Even if you do not realise it at the time, rejection can be a turning point that opens a world of new possibilities.

God created something out of nothing, and this is a great miracle that was about to happen. He created a whole new life out of the chaos and confusion of my life. That is the speciality of God. How great is that? The Holy Spirit hovered over the chaos before the creation at the very beginning of the book of Genesis.[72] He then intervened to bring order out of chaos. The Holy Spirit specialises in changing people's lives. He changes you into a different person like he did with Saul as He prepared him for the Kingship.[73] The person I am tomorrow will be different from the person I am today if I allow the Holy Spirit to change me. With the help of the Holy Spirit, I can constantly reinvent myself. The choices I make today will decide who I am tomorrow.

Most of my life had been spent following other people's thinking. Dogma would no longer be the deciding factor. That inner voice would no longer be drowned out by the views of others. As someone once said, *"Be yourself. Everyone else is taken."*[74] I would now filter out foreign voices in favour of God's voice speaking through scripture and my conscience.

---

72 Genesis 1:2

73 1 Samuel 10:6-10

74 This quote is attributed to Oscar Wilde, but there is no conclusive evidence that Oscar Wilde made this remark.

Taking Down the Flag of Rome

Spiritual abuse and all the other concerns tipped the scales. Had there been a firm sense of belonging to the Church, knowing that Catholicism was my spiritual home, it is doubtful that spiritual abuse alone would drive me away. Abuse was the issue that brought everything to a head. My discomfort with the whole status quo and now this, there was no way of staying.

Yet I did not feel mentally, financially, or strategically ready to leave at once. I left that parish and stayed with good friends until the church found a new parish for me to work in. I spent one more year in the Church before finally developing a strategy for transition. For the moment, mere survival superseded the desire to leave.

You will experience one of your most important moments in life when you finally muster the courage and certainty to give up what you cannot change. In situations where you cannot change the outcome, you must either accept the status quo and compromise, or you must change yourself. As a young man I wanted to change the Church, but finally decided that the only person I could change was myself. Maybe then I could make a difference with my life.

I always wanted to push myself to my limits, to realise my potential. The Church, on the other hand, this huge colossus of stability and champion of the status quo, is quite content with the way things are. I began to see the Church in the same way that Blackadder perceived Field Marshal Haig who, in his words, "*is about to make yet another gargantuan effort to move his drinks cabinet six inches closer to Berlin.*"[75]

---

75 Rowan Atkinson, *Blackadder Goes Forth* (https://inews.co.uk/culture/television/blackadder-quotes-161437)

I love producing new ideas for ministry and evangelism. In the Catholic Church, growing the Church and winning people to Christ were never on the agenda. In a marriage, couples can often find a solution in such differences. In my relationship with the Church, there was always only one side willing to change. I suppose a separation was inevitable.

I could no longer bear the thought of compromise and was unwilling to blame others. The conviction of the Holy Spirit was heavy on me. There was no way I could return to Ireland and place myself in the hands of the Church. That would mean allowing others to draft my story and live a fruitless life. The Holy Spirit had finally brought the Word of God home to my heart, and He would inspire me to write my own story. Instead of trying to change the Church, the change would start with myself.

The defining moment came in September 1983. I celebrated my last Mass, took down the flag of Rome and unofficially resigned from the Catholic Church. A lady called Margaret played an important part in this. She often visited me in the parochial house. She was a single woman who worked as a teacher and was constantly active in parish work.

Margaret might have detected my discontent and unhappiness. No one mentioned leaving the priesthood, but she suggested that I apply to a nearby teacher training college. This showed that my time had come. This would be the first step in my strategy to get free from the control of the higher-ups. Teacher training courses would start soon, but all the places had long been taken. Nevertheless, a position for religious studies became available and six candidates applied. I had to queue up and go for an interview. And guess what? They offered me the place.

The day I entered the teacher training college, I crossed the Rubicon. The decision was a particularly grave one that could not be changed. There would be no going back, and it would have significant outcomes.

I could not pay the course fees because I did not have the funds. The local council refused a grant application. Margaret persuaded me to apply for a judicial review. Subsequently, legal aid was granted, and the case was finally heard in the Law Courts in London on 12 November 1984. I won the case with costs awarded against the Department of Education and Science. It was reported in the Times newspaper and the Cork Examiner. The result meant that the council's original decision was in breach of EEC law. The Cork Examiner said the ruling *"could lead to more foreign students qualifying for English educational grants."*[76]

By the time the ruling came down, I had completed the college course and was already teaching. The council eventually reimbursed me for the fees. In addition, my own missionary society granted a loan during my studies, which, as it turned out later, did not have to be repaid. For this I am immensely grateful. I was blessed by the support that the Church gave me.

"Another world is not only possible, but she is also on her way. On a quiet day, I can hear her breathing."[77] For me, change was coming, it was *"breathing"* and was already living within me. It felt like I was leaving my own country. Catholics are my people, and even if you no longer live there, you stay connected and have an interest in affairs. In the truest sense of the word, my heart is still with Roman Catholics, like St Paul's attitude to his Jewish roots.

The next season in my life was way outside my comfort zone. Comfort zones are never your friend when it comes to change. An anonymous source says, *"If you want to change, you have to be willing to be uncomfortable"*.

---

76 Cork Examiner, 13th November 1984

77 Arundhati Roy, https://theysaidso.com/quote/arundhati-roy-another-world-is-not-only-possible-she-is-on-her-way-on-a-quiet-da

CHAPTER 9

NO MAN'S LAND

*In dark times we prove to ourselves
the power we did not know we had*

Change of Landscape

10 June 1977 is etched in my memory. As I climbed the steps to the altar (high table) the day after my ordination, it was a memorable experience. With the evening sunlight streaming in through the stained-glass windows, the church looked stunning in June.

Fast-forward seven years from the day of my ordination. The landscape had fundamentally changed. My 'vocation' had breathed its last. I was in a job that paid the bills, but I had no real enthusiasm for it. My passion and enthusiasm had disappeared like the mist over the River Shannon. The landscape had turned into a wilderness, a cold, frosty winter with not much warmth and little comfort. I was in no man's land. I left with nothing and was not in a relationship. I had to go back to the drawing board and start at the very beginning.

Arriving in Mansfield at the age of thirty-three to start my new job as a teacher, all my possessions were stowed in the back of 'Oscar', my little Fiat 127. This included my rocking chair. If that rocking chair had a memory, it would tell of the brokenness, the shattered dreams, and the inner emptiness.

I felt like I had lost my place in the universe. I now worked in a job that made me almost incapable of having feelings. This was not helped by a headteacher who 'carpeted' me for reminding him of a broken promise he had made to me when I was appointed. This man once again displayed a spirit of ownership, entitlement and control. I quickly found out that abuse also happens outside the Church.

I was surrounded by people, but all the conversations, banter and jokes were just noise to me. I joined in, but it meant nothing. The rocking chair would testify to the emotional numbness of my life at that time. Outwardly, no one would have noticed the inner turmoil I was going through.

What began with a party in 1977 ended with a funeral! What had begun with pomp and celebration now ended in a world of mourning. It had died and breathed its last, and there was nothing to replace it, at least not yet. I suppose you could say, "*I made a right hames of it.*"[78]

In my role as a teacher, I faced disrespect and rebellion daily, and I was constantly reminded of what a good life I enjoyed as a priest. I had to stand in front of an angry and rebellious class of fourteen-year-olds to be 'mooned' by a pupil. On another occasion a teenager sat at my feet and refused to budge even though there was an inspector in the room. I was not living; I was surviving. In fact, I had two full-time jobs – teaching and keeping my head above water.

---

78 I made a right mess of it.

Shame

This is not how it was supposed to end. Falling short of a lifelong commitment to the priesthood is considered a terrible failure from which one never recovers. The loss of face and the shame of making it public was even more painful. Not that I made it public, others did that for me. I could not bring myself to talk about it. When my separation became public, I at once felt devalued. I refused to think about what people might say and kept as far away as possible from people who knew me in my role as a priest. Let me say that people did not ostracise me, I did that to myself.

Going home was shameful, meeting the very people who had supported me and enabled my journey to priesthood. My heart was weighed down by the burden of estrangement. This was supposed to be a 'happily ever after' story – one of the biggest success stories the parish had ever experienced. Feeling shame and humiliation is a normal part of such a break-up. When you feel shame, all you want to do is crawl into a hole and save face. You are overcome with feelings of inadequacy as well as shame. I had violated the social norms of my community and as a result I felt untethered from my roots.

Despite the shame and humiliation, I had to take a long hard look at myself in the mirror and decide what was more important: to support a system I did not believe in, or to follow my inner voice? To avoid shame and humiliation, or to do the right thing? To lie down in failure, or to stand up and believe that I still had a calling from God? If I had not looked long and hard in the mirror, the world would now find me taking selfies with old ladies at Legion of Mary meetings. They would see me looking more than a little uncomfortable sprinkling holy water on objects. There would be a version of me at youth meetings, with long grey hair combed over and flossing to the words, "*I really care about the kids.*" What they would not see is the quiet desperation of someone who was dead on the inside. As I looked intently in the mirror, I had to decide, "*This is not for me!*"

Outcast

It is difficult for any priest to re-enter society as a lay person. During my time as a priest, I received a basic allowance, but when I left the priesthood, I had no money and I did not own a house, furniture, bank account or credit cards. I paid nothing into social security. I started from zero and had nothing saved for my retirement. At thirty-three, I was a beginner starting a new career.

In 1983, I took down the banner of the papacy. When I eventually applied for laicisation (returned to the lay state) I received a letter or dispensation from the Vatican. It said I was to avoid places where my former status was known. This dispensation was a confirmation that I existed outside the communal norm, something I had already experienced.

As an Irish citizen, you understand your identity will be an issue when you leave the priesthood and the Catholic Church. Since the foundation of the Irish state, Catholicism has been judged as the *sine qua non* of Irish identity.[79] You could not be fully Irish without being Catholic. This has been summed up humorously by Michael Redmond who said, "*Like most Irish people I was born Catholic. This came as a big shock to my parents, who were Jewish.*"[80]

79 William Olhausen, *On the rise and fall of the Irish Catholic Church*, https://www.oxfordhouseresearch.com/on-the-rise-and-fall-of-the-irish-catholic-church/, Posted on 19th March 2021

80 Des MacHale (Editor), *Wittypedia, Over 4,000 of the Funniest Quotations* (London, Prion, 2011), p.420

Somebody once confessed to being Jewish and was then asked, "*But are you a Catholic Jew or a Protestant Jew?*"

This form of Irish nationalism came about towards the end of the 19th century. It also attracted the Catholic hierarchy as well as the attention and support of Padraic Pearse. Pearse was the leader of the 1916 Easter Rising at the GPO in Dublin. The uprising was the spark for the struggle for Irish independence from the British. This event has been preserved in the Irish psyche as the greatest event in Irish history. Pearse's legacy has had a massive impact on Irish politics. To question Pearce in Ireland is like questioning Winston Churchill in Britain.

It was Pearse who marked Irish nationalism as distinctly Catholic. He expressed the idea that nationalism correlated to the Catholic Church. He wrote, "*Like a divine religion, national freedom bears the marks of unity, holiness, catholicity and apostolic succession.*"[81] The understanding that developed in the Irish psyche from this thinking was that God was not only Catholic, but He was also an Irish nationalist. God was on our side, and we had created God in our own image. Of course, God is not Catholic, Protestant, Irish or British. God is bigger than all that, and He is not exclusive to any religious or political group or tribe. If God is for anyone, He is for you and me and He is interested in humanity. God loved the world so much that he sent Jesus to die for humanity.[82] Let us not reduce Jesus to our national clique or our Christian tribe.

This Catholic version of nationalism excluded twenty five percent of the population who did not profess the Catholic faith. It successfully laid the

---

81 Padraic Pearse, *Ghosts* (Phoenix Publishing Company, Collected Works, 1924), p.226
82 John 3:16

foundation for the division of the state into North and South. Father Seamus Murphy put it concisely when writing about the 1916 Rising, "*Militarily insignificant, the Rising's political impact was large. It reinforced Ulster unionist determination to refuse all compromise with nationalists. It undermined John Redmond's Irish Parliamentary Party (IPP). To the present day, it has inspired IRA clones, to bomb Britain and unionists out of Ireland.*"[83] Had Pearse chosen a more democratic and non-sectarian path, Ireland would have turned out quite differently. Although Pearse is widely applauded, his initiative of violence was the pattern for the many violent attacks and campaigns by the Provisional IRA. In the years that followed, there were many such attacks, especially 'The Troubles', which lasted from about 1970 to 1998.

The nationalism I inherited is a very narrow and controlling form of identity. It made it difficult for me to give up Catholicism without seeming to give up my Irish identity as well. At best, I was perceived as less Irish and less patriotic. In Ireland, it is perfectly acceptable to be a non-practising Catholic. However, it is less acceptable to come out and say that you have left the Church and joined a different one, especially if you are a priest.

Among other things, I was dubbed 'West British.' This is a derogatory term for an Irish person who is perceived as English in terms of culture, religion, or politics. If you are called 'West British' by other Irish people, you are treated as an outcast. You are effectively excluded from your local community, which in my case was exclusively Catholic. It is very disturbing when your sense of national identity, of which you are immensely proud, is undermined. It pierces to the core of who you are.

---

83 Séamus Murphy SJ, *Dark Liturgy, Bloody Praxis: The 1916 Rising* (Studies, spring 2016, Volume 105, number 417), p.12

Attitudes in the Wilderness

The term 'wilderness' refers to an unfriendly, uncultivated, and isolated area. How would I cope with the isolation? This was another world that seemed so strange and alien. I felt out of place. The position of respect enjoyed by a priest as a valued member of the community was now history. This left big gaps in my life. These voids had to be filled. Every person who loses his identity must find out again who he is and what his life is about. That would take time.

It is easier said than done, but in these dark times we prove to ourselves the strength we did not know we had. The darkness and cold of winter drive us to find warmth. During this time I found warmth in my relationship with God and in my growing relationships with other Christians. I still had the embers of a fire inside me that needed to be rekindled. How long we stay in the desert depends on us and our attitude. It is important to keep our eyes on God through praise and thanksgiving and not to isolate ourselves from fellowship with others.

It is easy to give in to the 'blame game,' but I did not want to go there. I had to accept responsibility for where I was. Stephen Covey says that the first and most fundamental habit of an effective person is to be proactive which means taking responsibility for your life.[84] I was not going to blame my situation on circumstances or people in my past, no matter what had been said or done to me. I had to own my history as part of a conscious choice based on my values. I wanted my values to define my life, not my feelings of shame and inadequacy. This is where forgiveness and asking for forgiveness,

---

84 Stephen Covey, *The Seven Habits of Highly Effective People* (London, Simon & Schuster, 1989), p.78

honesty, truth, and transparency kicked in. I resolved to do the right thing, even though at times it bit me badly.

As Kevin Gerald writes, "*To replay yesterday is to lose today.*"[85] I had to stop looking back and focus on everything that was good about my new life. My former life still wanted to play the leading role, although it should not even have been an extra. For a long time, I was full of sadness, but over time I decided that while there were good things about my old life, I did not want it back. I knew what I missed and what I did not. As I found new relationships and a new ministry, the best and most valuable parts of my old life were integrated into my new situation. In this new life, the old feelings of love, safety and security were resurrected, but on a quite different level and in a vastly different way.

Others had devalued my currency. The imprint of other people's feet was all over me. I had been trampled underfoot like a crumpled five-pound note, and through my own fault. By this I mean that I had not cared enough for myself and had carelessly put myself in a vulnerable position by submitting to a legalistic structure that expected total allegiance in a way that Jesus would never have expected of me. But the wonderful thing about this 'fiver' is that it has not lost its value. No one will throw it away. You may have been trampled underfoot, but in God's eyes you still have the same value.

I worked in secondary schools for fourteen years, although I did not see this as my first calling. This was my 'no man's land,' but also the gateway to my new future. During what I call the fourteen-year hiatus, I wanted to return to ministry, but there was not an avenue to do that immediately. I gradually eased myself back into ministry, taking a two-pronged approach. While

85 Kevin Gerald, *The Proving Ground, The Nine Tests that Prove Your Personal Potential* (Tulsa, Oklahoma, Insight Publishing Group, 2003), p.61

pursuing a career as a teacher, I simultaneously took every opportunity to train and actively serve the vision of the pastor in my local church. In 1998, fourteen years after joining the movement, I was accepted as a recognised pastor in the Assemblies of God.

According to Napoleon Hill, an American self-help author, most people give up when faced with failure. In his classic book *Think and Grow Rich* he said, *"When defeat comes, accept it as a signal that your plans are not sound, rebuild those plans, and set sail once more toward your coveted goal."*[86] I concluded that my original plans from childhood had not been sound, so I chose to stand up and set sail again towards my goal. It has been said the definition of insanity is to do the same thing over and over while expecting a different result. It was time to stop making the same mistakes and so I pivoted in midstream.

At the point of leaving the priesthood, it seemed as if all the years of investment had been for nothing. If my life were a football match, I would be devastated by the score at half-time. But the game was not over yet, and the second half was still to come. Either I accept failure, or I go back to the drawing board and decide to stand up and fight for a new future.

---

86 Napoleon Hill, *Think and Grow Rich*, (Kindle Edition)

CHAPTER 10

A NEW FUTURE

"Surround yourself with people that reflect who you want to be and how you want to feel, energies are contagious."[87]

Cutting Down the First Tree

From a position of spiritual devastation, I experienced a remarkable and miraculous recovery, and by the power of God I was able to overcome an incredibly difficult situation. Once I let go of the unrealistic expectations of the cultic priesthood and accepted God's design for living, my life began to turn around. I can only marvel at God's goodness. My recovery was a process that had to be worked out in practical steps over many years. The seed of ministry planted in me as a child was still there, and I wanted to pursue that vision even though I had been led down a rabbit hole.

Noah's dream of building an ark to save humanity did not begin when the rain came. It began with hearing from God and then taking one small step. He started by cutting down the first tree, followed by many individual trees. Many people want to be part of the finished product, but how many are willing to cut down a forest of trees first? We want to receive God's provision,

---

87 Anonymous

but do we have the patience to take the small steps that will eventually make the dream come true?

Many Christians only move in their calling when they feel ready. The first time I preached in a Pentecostal church after leaving, I was not ready. I was still in a state of shell shock. It happened the year I was in the teacher training college. The congregation was small, but that did not help the nerves. Later I read a book *called Feel the Fear and Do It Anyway*[88] by Susan Jeffers. I preached regardless of my feelings, just as the book recommended. Waiting until you feel ready, anointed, and qualified is a recipe for procrastination.

Many of us want more money before we give. We will go to church when we feel we are good enough. Attending a small group can wait until we get more time. God may have spoken to us about taking on a task or ministry in the church but that will have to wait until we are fully prepared. The key to experiencing God's blessing on your money, your ministry and your future is to *"feel the fear and do it anyway."* Preaching the first time after I left was a small step, but it was the first of many, and it set a deliberate benchmark.

I am so glad that I was not surrounded by people who wrapped me in cotton wool, because then I would never have been able to face the realities of life, learn new skills and face new challenges. Yes, there were people who listened to me, but they were not 'enablers.'

---

88 Susan Jeffers, *Feel the Fear and Do It Anyway: How to Turn Your Fear and Indecision into Confidence and Action* (Vermilion, 2007)

Digging Deep

I dug deep and somehow found the resilience and strength to get my life going again. I had nothing but the grace of God working in me to rekindle the fire. People were not queuing up to give me advice, show me the way or give me a ministry position. In the beginning, there was no one to cheer me on. It was up to me now. There was no one to put food on the table, pay the bills, or do all the things that had been done for me before. I had to trust my inner voice now if I wanted to move forward. I must say that I am incredibly grateful for the ready meals and especially for the 'Vesta' curries that were part of my diet at the time!

Arriving at my Destination

Allow me to jump forward to the date that stands for a significant point of my ministry. The date was 4 July 2021. I was once again stepping out in front of a congregation, and I was stepping aside as the senior leader of the church that we had planted in 1996.

I had reached the age of seventy and knew it was time to step aside. In the twenty-five years that I had led the same church, I had given it my best shot. To quote another Irish phrase, "*I had given it a good lash.*" Things were not getting better under my leadership. I was no longer getting the same response or having the same impact. My passion and energy for the job were being challenged. More importantly, the church would suffer. When I am no longer bringing change, it is time for change. The church needed a new leader to bring fresh enthusiasm to take them beyond COVID and into the next season.

On that day in July, as I approached the podium, my feelings were a complete contrast to how I felt in my last days as a priest. Then I was alone and demoralised. Now, loving people surrounded me, many of whom had played a part in my recovery and helped me regain my self-respect. There had been many setbacks, but I was proud and happy because of the achievement of the team that surrounded me. It was a joy to see the faces of those who stood with me until the end of my shift. I felt a satisfaction that I had persevered, and the many challenges of ministry had not forced me to quit early. I am always encouraged and inspired when I read that Jesus loved to the end. John wrote in his gospel, *"It was just before the Passover Festival. Jesus knew that the hour had come for him to leave this world and go to the Father. Having loved his own who were in the world, he loved them to the end."*[89]

Even though I was relieved of the task the Lord had given me, it was still a privilege to remain in the same church and serve the vision in whatever way I could. Eventually, it is not about what we achieved or the work we did. It is not about position, promotion, or recognition. It is about love for God and love for each other. Ego is always at work when broken relationships result from the pursuit of position and recognition. It is better to drop the ego than to destroy a relationship. These friends, mentors, colleagues, and members loved the church to the very end and that was incredibly special.

This time I had not stepped up to an altar. I stepped up onto a platform and looked out at the congregation in front of me, all of whom had face coverings and were sitting at least a metre apart. My children, their spouses and grandchildren were all present. We gathered in the main hall of a building we renovated and built ten years earlier. It was more of a multi-purpose

---

89 John 13:1

community centre than a church, and it was accessible and open to the whole community.

There were no statues, pews, or confessionals in the main hall. This building was more representative of the kind of church I envisioned. This was not a 'one-man-band' church. It was not a place where we adopted a 'cultic priesthood model.' This church was based on gender equality, teamwork, servant leadership and respect for the gifts and contributions of everyone. The church was able to grow, flourish and function as a true community hub. And we did this in a former mining community.

We were also gathered for the handover service and the induction of my wife Liz into the leadership role of the church. This was a special event because there was a successor who continued the work. It is said that having *"a successor is the true measure of success."* I was enormously proud that Liz had the courage to put herself forward for the role. She had been with me through thick and thin. Both pain and joy were part of the experience of being in ministry throughout our marriage. And yet she was willing to stand out from the crowd and say, *"Here I am Lord, send me."* I am blessed in that I found a woman with whom I share the same core values that govern our beliefs and actions. There is no doubt that we are kindred spirits. When I was a priest, I dreamed of having such a woman by my side. We are of the same mind when it comes to serving God and the church. Without her attitude and outlook, Lifespring Church would not exist in its current form.

This gathering of people on 4 July 2021 was the culmination of thirty-seven years of God's provision in a different kind of church. It was certainly a demonstration of the extent to which God had changed me. I started with almost nothing, but I invited Jesus into my boat, and he filled it abundantly. My strategy of being patient and working on my dream, step by step, paid off. Anything worthwhile takes time. Every successful person who stands on the podium was once a beginner who refused to give up. God indeed made a way where there was no way.

God initiated and executed His 'new thing' through three remarkable encounters that turned my life around. Having highlighted the culmination of my recovery in ministry, I would now like to go back in time and recall these three remarkable encounters that God used to change my life for the better. I can only describe them as miracles. At the time I was not fully aware of their significance, but all three together proved the absolute faithfulness of God and the fact that God had not abandoned me.

Meeting a Man of God

As soon as I left the priesthood, I went on a spiritual quest to find a church that matched my beliefs. I had some ideas of what I was looking for. First of all, I knew what I was not looking for. I did not want a judgmental and legalistic church with a cold and unwelcoming spirit. Love is the only thing that can dispel the darkness so that you can flourish again. If you have ever felt like an outcast, you need to be accepted now.

The church I envisioned would derive its teachings from the Bible. I believed in a church where every member would be treated equally and encouraged to use their gifts and talents for the common good. My vision was a church where every believer had a personal relationship with Christ and was nurtured by Him in a genuine way. This would also be a church that preaches the gospel of Jesus Christ and actively recruits people to the cause of Christ. It would be a church in which the power and guidance of the Holy Spirit plays a vital role.

It never occurred to me to join a church with many single women so that I could find a wife. Although I felt ready for marriage before I left the priesthood, I now found it extraordinarily difficult to admit that I needed human companionship. When I was confronted with the reality of marriage, I realised that I had been conditioned to cope alone. In my current situation, I was neither able nor in any fit state to marry. My priority was to get well and get my life in order, not to get married.

I had been teaching for five months and had tried several churches. I was 'free' from bureaucracy and officialdom. In February 1985, I was invited to a gathering of Charismatic Christians at Mansfield Woodhouse Baptist Church. It was there that I met a tall, slender gentleman with curly hair and a broad grin. He introduced himself as Paul Johnson, the pastor of Blidworth and Rainworth Christian Fellowship. We struck up a conversation and I told him a little about my life and that I was looking for a new church. Paul did not hesitate and invited me to a small meeting of his fellowship the next Sunday. It was to take place in his own home.

At that time, I had no idea how momentous this invitation would be. It not only led me to discover my home church, but also the church in which I would marry my future wife. It was the church that inspired me to start what would later become Lifespring Church. This was no ordinary event. It was God's will and decision, and it was indeed "a door of hope." It was not a large church, but the people I met there were wonderful. To begin with, I did not trust anybody, and I stayed very much on the edge. Eventually, I discovered that energy is contagious. There is indeed a connection between the energy you receive from others and the results you achieve in your life. You must be mindful of those you allow into your life.

Things began to change when the church rented a community centre to do outreach. The evangelist arrived on time, but then became extremely ill and an ambulance had to be called. Paul decided to go to the hospital with him. His last words to me as he got into the ambulance were something like this: "*You will have to take over and preach. Take it from here.*" I had to stand in front of a crowd and spontaneously preach the gospel. After the sermon I called for a response and three people came forward to give their lives to Christ. It is always a great privilege to see people come to Christ. It was also wonderful that someone had put their trust in me.

The relationship with Paul and the church gave me the time I needed to heal and learn. During a fourteen-year hiatus whilst I was teaching in a school, I literally 'sat at the feet' of the man of God and learned a new way of ministry. Working with Paul opened up several new acquaintances and opportunities for me.

One cannot overestimate the importance of choosing the right church and moving with the right people. Everything began to change when my life began to synchronise with the life of this church. "*Show me your friends and I'll show you who you are,*" my mother used to say. "*Show me your friends and I'll show you where you are going,*" David Shearman later rephrased it. The book of Proverbs tells us, "*Walk with the wise and become wise, for a companion of fools suffers harm.*"[90] How true that is. It is not that I spent my time with bad people. I had taken my mother's advice and avoided bad company. The people I had moved with were good people, but they could not provide me with the guidance, vision, and strategy I needed to achieve my goal.

---

90 Proverbs 13:20

Meeting My Future Wife

A legacy is anything that stays behind after a person or event has passed away. The chapter of the priesthood in my life ended, but it left a legacy. The promise of celibacy I had taken was part of that legacy. As I began to recover my self-esteem, I began to think about marriage and having children. But I could not shake the feeling that marriage would mean disobedience to God. I will come to that later. If I could overcome this obstacle, the next step would be to find the right person. In fact, it transpired the other way round. I found the right person first.

It was Dales Bible Week 1984 and I had just been hired as a religious education teacher at a school near Mansfield. The church that was pitched across the road from me happened to be from Mansfield. This was no coincidence, but a divine intervention. A young woman in sawn-off jeans, clearly a member of that church, was walking around shooting a water pistol at people. Her name was Liz, and she was to be my future wife.

After learning that I was on my way to Mansfield, the church took me under their wing. The ladies even helped me find accommodation. "*I have just met a very nice young man,*" one of the ladies, affectionately known as Aunty Sylvia, told Liz. Sylvia was match making in her inimitable way.

I met Liz again when I joined Paul Johnson's fellowship the following February. Liz had changed churches a few months earlier. We spent the next four months in the same fellowship as church colleagues. Liz then moved to Cardiff after getting a job at the YMCA. She returned a year later and moved in with a family just around the corner from where I had bought a house. We became friends and I remember playing squash together.

Our romance was sparked by a car crash, curry and burnt onions. Liz's twin sister was learning to drive that summer. She had borrowed her brother's car to go bowling in Nottingham with a group of friends and she needed the services of a qualified driver. I was entrusted with this task.

Everything went smoothly until the return journey. Liz's sister misjudged the length of a parked bus when she tried to overtake it. She clipped the bumper and scratched the side of her brother's car. I am sure Liz's sister could have delivered the message herself, but that task fell to Liz and me. Her brother was fine with it, and I later found out that the car belonged to his father. But that is not the aspect of the evening that was particularly important. I remember that evening best because I invited Liz over for a curry as we stood talking on the street, having delivered the news about the damage to the car. Unfortunately, I burnt the onions. That was the beginning of our romance, sparked by a car crash, curry, and burnt onions.

Everyone believed we should get married. I was struggling with the fact that I had taken a promise of celibacy. I had left the Catholic Church, but the Church had not left me. Outwardly I was living a new life, but inwardly I was living in the mindset of the old. Layers of thought still had to be stripped away. Ideas surfaced such as, "*You should not get married. You have taken a promise of celibacy and God will hold you to it. You will lose your freedom and independence to minister wherever God calls you.*" I had not yet come to terms with the fact that I was dead to my old, conditioned way of thinking, and it would take time and some unique events to break the deadlock.

Paul Johnson came to me one day and said that David Shearman wanted to see me in his office. David was pastor of a large church in Nottingham and a nationally known figure in British Assemblies of God. I learned that he wanted to talk to me about my relationship with Liz. He asked me if I loved her. I told him that I did. David must have sensed hesitation and then politely suggested that I become organised and that it was okay to get married. It was reassuring to hear David's advice. Later, however, I received an added confirmation that sealed the whole thing for me.

The affirmation I was looking for came four years after I left the priesthood, and it came in a remarkable way. I had an on-again, off-again relationship with Liz. Liz knew exactly what she wanted, but that was not the case with me. When she came to see me one night, we were in the 'off season' of our relationship. I was a keen fan of tropical fish, and she came to look at the new school of baby guppies that had just arrived. We sat and talked while admiring the baby fish.

As we sat there talking, that inner voice said to me in no uncertain terms, *"Ask her to marry you!"* *"What are you talking about? Are you sure? Do you mean right now?"* was my reaction. Even though I never heard the voice again on that subject, its power convinced me to act immediately.

With no ring to offer and not even thinking of getting down on one knee, I at once popped the question in front of the fish tank as we sat side by side. *"Liz, will you marry me?"* I asked. There! I said it, and that was the breakthrough. It wasn't as if the thought had never crossed my mind before. Liz was open mouthed and looked at me with a stunned look on her face. *"Excuse me?"* was her response. I repeated the proposal. As soon as she realised that I was serious, she did not think twice and said, *'Yes.'* I promised to call her at work the next day and we would go shopping for an engagement ring at lunchtime.

When Liz woke up the next morning, she was still unsure. This was not surprising given the unusual nature of the proposal. Was she dreaming? Did it really take place? *"Did he really ask me to marry him?"* The only thing that could reassure her was the phone call I promised to make. This would confirm to her that she had not imagined anything. Of course, I called, and we arranged to go and buy a ring during her lunch break.

I now felt emboldened and had a divine imperative to get married. This nullified any other law or Church rule. At the Council of Trent, the Catholic Church imposed binding anathemas (curses) on any priest who abandoned celibacy or refused to ask God for the gift. In the eyes of the Church, it was sacrilege to marry. But now I had final confirmation that everything the reformers and my advisors said about celibacy had hit the mark.

Liz and I at once began wedding preparations. Six months later we were married. The sky did not fall in and there was no sign whatsoever that God was displeased. On the contrary, the opposite was true. God began to release his blessings on our lives in a wonderful way.

Having married Liz in 1988, we both got fully integrated into the life and ministry of the church. Then in 1994, Paul Johnson commissioned us to do some work with a house group in Ollerton. This work was progressing well, and new members were joining. Paul began to teach and preach about planting a new church, and so the work at Ollerton developed into a public meeting in 1996 which formed a second congregation of Blidworth Church.

Out of this new future that God gave me came the fulfilment of a vision that I had harboured for over twenty years. My ultimate aim over those years was to be a church planter. This was happening imperceptibly step by step. The house group grew into a congregation which then developed into an autonomous Assemblies of God church in its own right.

CHAPTER 11

A NEW CHURCH

"You can be committed to the Church but not committed to Christ, but you cannot be committed to Christ and not committed to the Church."[91]

Meeting God

Love for God and others is essential for a healthy church. After I discovered the presence of a loving church in my life, no one could convince me that church could be just an optional extra. If you love Christ, then you will also love His church. If I had isolated myself from a healthy, bible believing, Spirit filled church, I would still be living in insecurity and self-hatred. I discovered that God works through loving people.

In 1998 I had another significant encounter with the Lord in which He spoke to me this time about the church. This encounter with God was the third important encounter that not only confirmed a new direction but set me on the path to founding a new church.

As I sat at my kitchen table, my inner voice said to me, *"I want you to build a church in Ollerton."* The voice was an unmistakable sign that the work in Ollerton would develop into a church in its own right and not just a congregation of another church.

---

91 Joel Osteen

While I listen to my inner voice, I also believe in submitting what I am hearing to other trusted leaders. I decided to present my 'proposal' to Paul and the elders. I must say that I did this with trepidation, not knowing what the response would be. I had resolved in advance to respect their decision and not to go it alone. As it turned out, the response was unanimous and incredibly positive and encouraging. With great wisdom, the elders set a timetable during 1999 for preparations leading up to the launch of the new church. The new church was founded on 1 January 2000, the first day of the new millennium.

These three encounters were crucial to my recovery and helped me make a successful transition from priest to pastor. These meetings were the foundation stone for the establishment of a new church in Ollerton. Over twenty-five years, I led the church through various phases or seasons in the life of this community.

1. The Planting Season

The first season in Ollerton was spent planting the church, which took place between 1996 and 1999. The church began as a small house group that quickly expanded. It was a group of capable people who had not yet learned to work together as a team.

In the first year, the wheels almost came off the waggon. There was unrest and whispering in the congregation; it became clear that some people were unhappy with my leadership style and were attempting a 'coup.' I would have been overwhelmed and overrun if I had to fight this battle alone. Fortunately, my sending Pastor Paul Johnson helped repel the attack. I remember well the showdown meeting in the autumn of 1997. The decisive moment had come, and we would find out whether we would succeed or be a complete failure. Paul asked the crucial question, *"Are you with us or not?"* This was a very incisive question and led to some people leaving the church. However, it was encouraging to see so many people standing with us.

2. The Growing Season

This 'pruning' experience germinated the seed of growth. It welded us into a team that ushered in the growing season. Those who surrounded me during this season proved to be excellent allies. There were no prima donnas here, just a group of people united by a common vision. We were all willing to make sacrifices to win people for Christ and to grow the church. To accommodate the growth, we had to move our Sunday service several times.

While we cannot repeat or replicate what happened more than twenty years ago, it is important to remember that the fundamental principles for growth and success are still the same. These include unity of vision, a spirit of agreement, mutual respect and hard work. Most important of all is being called and empowered by the Holy Spirit. This list is by no means exhaustive! In the first season, there was undoubtedly a lack of unity and agreement. On certain occasions, respect was also lacking. This scenario was reversed during the growing season.

The Alpha course played a huge role in the growth of the church in this season and following. We linked up with national evangelists Roy Todd and Barry Woodward. We held Sunday morning evangelistic events such as 'Breakfast Gems'. This was a service with a breakfast and a topical message. We saw many people sign up to become Christians.

In this second phase, we also developed a social action programme under which we started distributing food parcels to the vulnerable. We opened a charity shop, developed an outreach programme for drug users and started a youth group. This phase created the initial good practice policies and procedures for the larger programme we undertook during COVID-19.

We know that the seeds of what we are doing today were sown over twenty years ago. From helping one family with food hampers in 1998, this small beginning has generated a whole series of acts of kindness in the present day. These initiatives include a food bank (CAR Project) which has given out 200,000 meals to vulnerable people in North Nottinghamshire since COVID-19 began. We opened the Oasis Café which is a training café for disabled people. We run a memory café for people with Alzheimer's. We also operate 'Energise', a club for children aged 5-17. Framework supplies a service around benefits and getting back into work. Weightwatchers is also on site, as is Ollerton Friendship Club, a social club offering refreshments, bingo, socialising, and outings for seniors. The centre is open for four hours on Tuesday evenings and serves free food for those who want to keep warm and keep their bills down. Make Lunch, a club that fills the hunger gap for children receiving free school meals, takes place during school holidays. In addition, the COVID vaccination hub has been using the centre for almost two years. There is a social bingo club, and we host a NAAFI (Navy, Army, Air Force Institute) breakfast and an autism club. The aim of running or encouraging these groups is to combat isolation and help people with their mental health.

3. The Construction Season

Behind all the good that happens in life, God is at work. It may not be obvious to us, but with the eyes of faith we can see the presence of God. His presence is seen in people, in circumstances and in giving us the means to overcome great obstacles. We may not immediately say, "*That was a miracle*," but underneath it all, God is at work, showering His approval on our efforts.

The third season was such a season. It was the season of building, mergers, acquisitions and further numerical growth. It was heralded by a marvellous event in early 2005. It was a clear sign from God that He was present in our work.

There was another Assemblies of God congregation in town, and we had talked several times about joining together, but for assorted reasons we had put the idea on hold, unable to make it happen, at least at that time. Then, one evening in February 2005, I received a call at about 9.00pm from Pastor Robert Day, the leader of the other church. His leadership team wanted Liz and me to come to a meeting they were holding. We were baffled as to why they wanted a meeting at that time of night.

When we arrived full of curiosity, Robert wasted no time. "*We want you to take over our church and we will give you our building on Sherwood Drive so we can all move in together,*" he said. "*There are no conditions, and we expect nothing in return from you. We will serve your leadership.*"

I was speechless and did not know what to say. The idea of churches splitting has been commonplace in our lifetimes, but churches joining together, well, that was almost unprecedented. Under Paul Johnson's ministry at Blidworth, we had experienced a similar miracle when Blidworth and Rainworth Christian Fellowship merged with Blidworth Pentecostal Church to form Sherwood Forest Community Church. After consultation with our leadership team, we of course gratefully accepted Robert's offer and held our first meeting together on Easter Sunday 2005.

The merger of the two churches gave us the means to enter the building season. The merger was a great blessing and opened our community to all kinds of new possibilities. The old Methodist church we had inherited from Pastor Robert was renovated and a new foyer and main hall added.

We went through a long planning and funding process for the new building project. Our preferred funder did not want to fund the church but wanted to fund a new company called Global Community Connect (GCC), which we had set up in 2009 for community outreach. The church granted GCC a one hundred-and twenty-five-year lease on the building. The funder then gave GCC a loan and a grant to complete the work. This was a miracle in itself, seeing that this new company had never traded and had no financial records. The £250,000 loan was to be repaid over ten years. The church was given the right to use the building for its spiritual work. The situation was not ideal, but it provided the church with the facilities it needed for its work.

We completed the new building and renovation of the old part in 2012. The benefits of a new building are fantastic. The new main hall is a multi-purpose room shared by the church and community which accommodates up to one hundred and eighty people. We have a training room, a meeting room and office space. One of the wishes expressed by the church and community was for a café, and we delivered on that.

There were times before and during the building season when it looked as if we would not finish the project. But then we experienced God's incredible help in answer to our prayers. The eventual outcome of the project far exceeded what the church could afford. God blessed a small community in a former coal mining area in an amazing way. Due to the closure of the mine, many community facilities in the town had been closed. In response to the prayers and faithfulness of a community of believers, God blessed not only the church but also the town.

Many former coal mining communities in this area feel forgotten and neglected. It can be tempting for churches to feel that these communities are too difficult to work in. Bethel Music and Jenn Johnson released the song 'Goodness of God'[92] in 2019. Unlike many who believe God has forgotten us, this song speaks of the incredible goodness of God, declaring, "... *all my life You have been faithful. And all my life You have been so, so good."* It is important to proclaim the goodness and faithfulness of God not only about the church, but also about the community in which we live. God has a plan, not only for individuals, but also for communities.

The construction work on the building was to begin in less than three months. At this point, our solicitor contacted us and informed us that we did not own part of the land on which we wanted to build. This put the whole project in jeopardy.

The footprint of the building was very tight, and we could not build without this piece of land. The church had 'bought' the land ten years earlier, but it had not been properly recorded at the Land Registry. We did not own the land! This required last minute negotiations with the owners. They demanded a lot of money, knowing how valuable the land was to us. We called this plot of land the 'ransom strip.' Finally, we reached an agreement, and the project was saved.

The funding deadline was 31 March 2011 and the conditions for funding were to sign a contract with a contractor and break ground before the funds could be released. We had to sign a contract worth half a million pounds,

---

92 The song was from the album Victory and was written by Ed Cash, Ben Fielding, Jason Ingram, Brian Johnson, and Jenn Johnson. Song was produced by ED Cash.

even though the money was not yet in our bank account. After a review, the Church Council decided that the risk was worth it. We put our trust in God and the funders. We signed the contract, broke ground and sure enough, the money arrived. It was the biggest risk we ever took as a church, but it paid off.

4. The Storming Season

The overall outcome of forming two governance structures was never an easy arrangement and the eight years following the building project were difficult. There was always tension between the visions of GCC and the church. The building phase was followed by the storming phase.

During this season, we had to weather the storm, and this was a very trying time and things could easily have gone pear shaped. The storming season was sparked off by different ideas about how the building should be used and what kind of café we wanted. The consultation we did said the community wanted a 'community café,' but some felt we should be aiming for an upmarket cafe. We stuck with the idea of a community café as running an upmarket café would not be in keeping with the demographics of the community.

To get through this season, everyone had to familiarise themselves with their role in the church and in the centre and how they relate to the other team members. Everyone knows the challenge of coordinating a team. We had to coordinate different teams in two governance structures that interacted with each other. The more complex the arrangement, the more likely it is that there will be conflict.

In the years of austerity that followed the opening of the building, it was always a struggle to raise the money for the ten-year mortgage at the end of each month. This caused us some headaches and was certainly a cause for concern during that stormy period. The lender agreed to extend the term, but we were still struggling. We were under pressure to always come up with new initiatives to bring in money, but we never failed to meet our obligation to pay the mortgage.

Then, we had a memorable meeting with the lender's representative where God gave us an incredible breakthrough. We had been talking about new fundraising initiatives for several years. The lender made a proposal that was 'outside the box.' If we could raise £100,000, the loan company would write off the remaining £100,000 that we still owed. The loan would be paid off if we could raise the money. But where were we to get this amount of money? The answer was simple! Go to another lender and apply for a mortgage. So we approached Kingdom Bank, who gave us a 25-year mortgage of £100,000 to repay the lender. The repayments were affordable and that took all the pressure off us.

We were now free of any obligations to the original lender. The next step was to achieve a unified vision in our structure. This was something I always wanted, but we took a circuitous route to get there. Unity came about on 1 August 2020 when GCC, that was now called Lifespring Centre, and Lifespring Church merged into a single entity called Lifespring Church and Centre.

An old cliché that one hears repeatedly in the churches is the reproach: "*You are always looking for money.*" I have never made a secret of the fact that the Church needs money. I always explained to our congregation that our mission is to change lives. I would challenge people to share in the joy of giving to achieve our mission. It is expensive to construct a new building and renovate an existing one. A comfortable place to sit and a warm building cost money. Reaching out to the community, feeding the hungry, running clubs and ministries and paying staff are just some of the many things that need to be financed..

We developed a funding strategy that goes beyond relying on the donations of the congregation. The money for the building project came from finding the right funders and applying for grants and loans. We became quite good at writing funding applications and most of the funds for our building project were raised through funding bids. This is a skill that is learned over many years and many failed applications. Every failure is an opportunity to learn something new about writing bids.

We developed several funding streams to finance the day-to-day running of the new community hub. We opened new charity shops and a trading café, which has now become a training café for people with disabilities. We receive rent and service charges from projects and community groups that use the building, not to forget donations from the congregation. All of this helps to pay for salaries and the running and maintenance of the church.

A bright spot towards the end of the fourth season was the merger between Lifespring and Bethel Church at Church Warsop. It came unexpectedly. Pastor Joy Troop, pastor of Bethel, visited me at the end of September 2017 to tell me that the time had come for them to close the church at Church Warsop and sell the assets. It is never a good thing when churches are closed. I suggested the possibility of Lifespring taking over responsibility for Bethel. Joy agreed, because she did not want the church to close either. A brief time later the merger took place, and the two churches entered a happy marriage.

The great marvel that came out of this merger was the marriage between Pastors Robert Day and Joy Troop. The two mergers in 2005 and 2017 had brought them together in the same church in a way that would not have been possible otherwise. Both had lost their spouses in the intervening years, and the mergers united not only the churches but the pastors. They were married on 29 August 2022 and remain valued members at Lifespring.

5. The COVID Season

The final season, during my tenure as pastor, was the COVID season. COVID-19 certainly caused the church to plateau. A plateau can occur when you must focus on other things. In the three years leading up to 2019, we had at least ten major crises to deal with, and this was followed by the challenges posed by COVID-19. While it is important not to take your eye off the ball, momentum is inevitably slowed down when a pandemic hits, people try to usurp your leadership or do things that affect the morale of the church. But that does not have to be the end, it can be the gateway to the next stage. We are now entering the next season after the pandemic when the Lord is breathing new life into us.

A strong feature of the new Lifespring Church was a commitment to missions. Having spent three years as a missionary in Ghana, it was natural for me to have an affinity with that country. However, we progressed to develop a relationship with Indigenous churches in a number of countries.

CHAPTER 12

HEART FOR MISSION

"But you will receive power when the Holy Spirit comes on you;
and you will be my witnesses in Jerusalem, and in all Judea
and Samaria, and to the ends of the earth."[93]

Instead of giving money to large organisations working abroad, our strategy was to support our own missionaries or build relationships with individual indigenous pastors.

Supporting our own Missionaries

In 2015 Liz and I made a memorable trip to visit our missionary family in Southeast Asia. The family had set out there in 2014 to answer God's clear call to be involved in Bible translation. When we visited them, they were in the capital city learning the language and acclimatising to the culture. Their progress in learning the language was impressive and their children seemed to be adjusting well to their new environment.

I remember visiting a village in the north of the country where a European couple was involved in a translation initiative. The majority of the population

---

93 Acts 1:8

lives in villages, and we were able to experience first-hand the challenges faced by missionaries and local Christians. We learned about the mixture of Buddhism and animism that makes up the traditional religion of the country. Christians have to overcome the feeling that becoming a Christian is in some ways a betrayal of their national identity. We learned of individual Christians who were put under massive pressure by their families to sacrifice to false gods in times of crisis.

A few years before the family went on mission, they visited me and the leadership to share their vision. They said they had been praying about it and it had been burning in them for a long time. We encouraged them to contact Wycliffe Bible Translators, who accepted them after a rigorous process. They were encouraged to attend a Bible school to prepare themselves.

As their home church, we still partner with this family and rejoice that our church's passion for mission is having an impact on countries far beyond our borders. My passion is partnership, and it has been great to work with Assemblies of God and Wycliffe to make their vision a reality.

Visit in 1993

Based on our strategy of working with individual ministries, Pastor Paul Dsane from Takoradi visited my home church at Blidworth in 1992. This was the beginning of a long and fruitful relationship that led to me making six short-term mission trips to Africa in the following years.

During the month-long visit to Ghana in 1993, I must have preached forty times and visited many churches and towns. The doors for ministry opportunities opened by themselves. My earlier experiences of Ghana were invaluable. I always started my sermons in the local language, and that endeared me to the congregation at once. When I did this, it was as if people's hearts melted, and we had an instant connection. I had great freedom to pray with people and saw many people converted to Christ and baptised in the Holy Spirit.

Paul Dsane and I talked about how our two churches could work together to help the people of Takoradi. Our meeting was the catalyst for the establishment of a Bible School, a series of 'cottage Industries' and eventually a medical clinic in one of the rural areas that served many villages. I remember returning to Ghana in 1996 with a team of people who had suitcases packed with various dyes for the newly emerging tie-dye industry. We taught at the Bible school, which was already up and running.

The vision of the clinic was realised in 2010 when a group from different churches visited Ghana. Pastor Paul Johnson and I opened the clinic in a formal ceremony with much pomp and festivity. The clinic cost about £80,000 to build and was funded by charity shops and generous donations from churches and individuals. Lifespring contributed almost half of this amount. This was a fantastic achievement considering that the church desperately needed money to fund its own building project.

Various Mission Trips

In 2002 I went on a trip to Ghana and Burkina Faso with Pastor Stephen Earnshaw from Nottingham. We took an exceedingly long bus journey from Kumasi to Ouagadougou in Burkina Faso. When we arrived at the border we got into trouble. We accidentally photographed the local police station, which is illegal in Ghana. In front of some high-ranking police officers, we were accused of being spies. I tried to explain that we were ministers of religion and had no bad intentions. The police officer replied, *"If you are a minister, you know everything. You should know that you are not allowed to take pictures."* They took our cameras and were about to rip out the film. I did what a Ghanaian would do in that situation: I begged! That seemed to work. They gave us back our cameras and we were allowed to leave with a warning.

This reminds me of another memorable trip taken years later with my friend David Littlewood. David is an accredited Assemblies of God minister, and we were on a preaching tour of some churches. It was the bus trip from hell. Tamale was our destination, a 340-mile journey. We had reserved seats on a luxury coach, but when the coach arrived it was anything but luxurious. The seats were hard as brass, and I had to reposition myself every few miles to find a more comfortable position.

The bus set off, making many detours through towns and villages. People came and went with their goods – the contents of their market stalls, farm produce and sometimes even live animals. It was not surprising that every now and then an argument broke out. There was something unpredictable about the whole journey.

We had not been on the road long when it became clear that this bus was not up to the task. We were on this beautiful road that the Chinese had built. The bus started chugging and slowed down. It broke down, but the driver was able to get it going again. However, from that point on, it broke down repeatedly. We were only moving at a snail's pace and were several hours behind schedule. It was already late in the day as we headed north, but the problem was getting worse. Would we have to spend the night on the bus, surrounded by mosquitoes? The bus finally gave up and refused to go any further.

The engine was under the floor in the passenger compartment. One of the new passengers appeared as our 'saviour' and said he could fix it, but he needed tools. He disappeared into a nearby village. After some delay, he returned with a spanner and tools and started his work. The bus finally started up again and took us to our destination, albeit many hours late. This kind gentleman was the nearest thing to the AA that we came across. Experiences like this leave an indelible impression of Africa, its unpredictability, its people, customs, and roads.

One of the highlights of returning to Africa for me was being able to take my son Daniel with me in 2008. We preached at Paul Dsane's church at Takoradi and in many other churches as well.

I remember visiting a town called Asankrangwa in the heart of the Western Region. This town is very rural, and we travelled for many hours on dusty, rutted roads to get there. We stayed in a hotel where we had to convince the hotel management that we were father and son and therefore only needed to rent one room. It was the hotel's policy not to let same-sex couples stay in the same room.

On this trip we also visited Kakum National Park, whose landscape is 90% tropical forest. The park is one of three places in Africa where an elevated treetop walkway leads through the forest. The walkway stretches 1,150 feet (350 m) above the forest floor and offers a bird's eye view and a great chance to see some of the wildlife below. We did not see any elephants, monkeys or exotic birds, and Daniel was disappointed because he wanted to see monkeys. You must go further into the forest to have any chance of seeing them. However, the trek above the trees was exciting and spectacular.

We also visited Elmina and Cape Coast Castles where our guide recalled some of the worst excesses of the Portuguese, Dutch, and British Empires. These castles were centres of the slave trade. It was harrowing to hear how the slaves were treated and to see the crowded, unhygienic, unlit, and airless conditions in which they were kept prisoner. We visited a dungeon where up to four hundred shackled male slaves were kept in the most appalling conditions.

We saw the balcony where the governor stood to select one of the four hundred female slaves gathered below as his 'sex slave' for the day. After raping them, the terrified women were given a proper meal and their first wash since their capture.

Those who survived illness and the terrible living conditions were sold to slave owners across the Atlantic. We were led to the 'Door of no Return,' a door that led directly from the castle to a waiting ship that would take the slaves on the dangerous journey across the sea. As we stood there at the door, looking out to sea, we could feel the hopelessness and despair of the people whose lives had been snatched away. These castles were the last sight the slaves had of their homeland before they were shipped off never to see their families and homes again.

In summary

During my many years of travelling to Africa, the number of people who wanted to become Christian was phenomenal, and I had the privilege of leading many to Christ. The barrenness and poverty in the lives of the people was balanced by the living water of God's presence. While Westerners try to remedy their unhappiness with being busy, material things, friendships or status, Africans seek to be sustained by the living water that never runs dry.[94]

---

94 John 7:37–39

In the next chapter I want to write about the course corrections I made to get where I wanted to go. It was only through these rather sweeping changes that I was able to set out into a new future and plant a new church.

CHAPTER 13

COURSE CORRECTIONS

"Two roads diverged in a wood, and I-
I took the one less travelled by,
And that has made all the difference."[95]

For some people, course correction is quite a smooth affair. If a plane is off course, a slight course correction can put the plane back on course. For me, life was like a train heading for a specific destination. What was required of me was the radical change of getting off that train and getting on a completely new train on a different track. That was quite radical, but it had far-reaching effects.

In a way, I packed two lives into one. Confucius is reported as saying, *"You have two lives, and your second one begins when you realise you only have one."* I realised that I had only one life, but my life had two halves. I had to decide how best to live the second half. The necessary course corrections would require a profound, one might say seismic, shift in direction.

I reached a stage in life where I had to remain true to my convictions. In Shakespeare's play Hamlet, Polonius gives his son Laertes advice on how to behave at university. He says, *"This above all: to thine own self be true, And*

---

95 Robert Frost, *The Road Not Taken* (The Atlantic Monthly August 1915)

it must follow, as the night the day, thou canst not then be false to any man.[96] This advice today means to be uncompromisingly true to oneself and is often quoted as undeniably reliable. However, no person is an island, and we are always influenced in some way by others. I have found that Shakespeare's saying is only reliable when the presence of Christ and His Word in you, is given space to shape your convictions. You find your true self when you find Christ and allow His Word to be *"a lamp for my feet, a light on my path."*[97]

I have indeed chosen a road *"less travelled by"*. Walking the path that few others walk is extraordinarily difficult and unsettling. I had to correct bad decisions, make many course corrections and leave many things behind.

Separation

So the first correction was very painful. It meant that I had to separate myself from the unique 'band of brothers' to which I belonged by the laying on of the bishop's hands. I was not only parting with an organisation, but also with friends and colleagues. Despite the pain, it was right to part with this priestly status, which in many circles is considered higher and purer than the status of the ordinary Catholic. I left a church that reduces people in the pews to a subordinate role and elevates priests to a privileged class. I left a church that placed the clergy in a lofty and untouchable position and protected reputations at all costs. I left behind compulsory celibacy and the control that the church hierarchy exercised over me.

---

96 Shakespeare, *Hamlet,* Act I, Scene 3
97 Psalm 119:105

The pain of separation hit me when my mother died shortly after Christmas 1985. This happened a year after I started teaching. I separated myself to such an extent that I did not tell my family my address. They knew the area where I lived, and I only found out that my mother was dying when the police came looking for me. I returned to Ireland and had the privilege of praying for her before she died. I was the only one present at her death. I attended the funeral and recall going to the 'wake' in civilian clothes. There, the loss of social status hit me hard. Normally, I would have been the one to lead the funeral.

Inner Voice

Another big course correction was being guided by my inner voice and not by the teaching authority (Magisterium) of the Church. I personally have no witness that the teaching authority of the Church is infallible or inspired by the Holy Spirit. I am not setting myself up as another pope because my source of infallibility is the Bible. I do not claim any special enlightenment in this matter, but I can only claim to speak for God as far as my beliefs and practice echo the biblical texts. I have no personal agenda against the Church and claim no moral superiority, but I do point out any teaching as far as it is not Bible based.

My inner voice led me to my home church. The Bible does not tell you which church to join, but it does give guidance on what a New Testament church looks like. I found that the church, and in particular some people in it, carry God's presence in a way that regularly releases healing. Paul Johnson was certainly one such man. In other words, I found a church with a life-giving platform. This church imparted grace, not judgement or condemnation. This was simply by being present and sitting under the ministry and listening to the Word of God with an open heart. As a result, I experienced a miraculous restoration as a member of that church. When I joined, I had no confidence. When I was sent out to plant a church at the end of my time there, I had the confidence of the leadership and they felt I was healthy enough to lead my own ministry. This is the power of a loving Bible-believing fellowship.

It was my inner voice that led me into marriage. Again, the Bible does not tell you who to marry, but it does lay out clear principles for a Christian marriage relationship.

It is this inner voice that guides me in my daily life and pastoral ministry. When it comes to doctrinal or ethical issues, my inner conscience guides me, especially when the Bible is silent on these issues. When you open the Bible and a verse catches your eye, you should listen up and take note of it. God wants to show you something.

In the ministry there were many occasions when I was very much conflicted about the solution to pastoral problems and conundrums. The solution came either through the words of my mentor, John, or after a time of prayer and Bible study. I would experience a moment of revelation in which I could see the solution crystal clear. It was as if a curtain had been pulled back and the solution leapt out at me.

Culture

Although I resisted the culture of the Catholic Church, I was faced with an impossible task. However, the new path I took gave me the opportunity to help shape the culture of a local church rather than a global corporation.

It was a much more achievable goal. Paying attention to the culture of the church became central to my work as a pastor. I took seriously what was encouraged or discouraged, allowed or rejected in our church. Culture is really revealing when you see it in action. From the beginning we said we wanted to be a 'warm, welcoming and worshipful church.' This was the kind of culture we wanted to encourage.

You see culture when you enter a church, in the way people greet or ignore each other, talk to each other, and take time for each other, especially the guests. It manifests in how often people show up and if they show up on time. Culture is seen in the way people interact with each other during worship and in the 'rituals' of the church.

The way people respond to leadership is an important indicator of culture. Whenever I noticed a lack of response in the congregation, I asked myself, *"Am I promoting the wrong thing?" or "Is there a culture problem here?"* When I noticed that an evangelism event was met with little response, I concluded that we had a culture problem. To change the culture, I needed to address some issues within myself and our leadership team. Are we living the values we expect others to embrace? Are our sermons and messages in line with the values we promote? Do we show that this is a priority by investing our time, gifts, and money? Do we celebrate those who promote our values and are getting the job done? We did not always get the perfect results, but we needed to make sure we were moving in the right direction.

For a culture to be relevant to contemporary society, it must be dynamic. So, while the gospel message never changes, culture is constantly evolving. Some churches try to keep the *status quo* and therefore lose their relevance and no longer connect with society. However, pastors of growing and thriving churches pay careful attention to the culture of their church because it is the catalyst for growth or decline.

Vision

We become the ideal we see in our minds and the vision we carry in our hearts. As Winston Churchill said, *"The empires of the future are empires of the mind."* Mental vision captures what is not yet real or present. Jonathan Swift said, *"Vision is the art of seeing things invisible"*. Since childhood, I carried the vision in my heart to become a priest and after many years this dream was finally unveiled.

However, the absence of a dynamic and ongoing vision caused me to fall into dissatisfaction and discouragement. In fact, I hit a brick wall. I was disconnected from what I truly wanted which was not just to be a minister or priest, but to minister in a church with a life-giving platform.

As I began to associate with dynamic leaders, a new ideal and vision took shape in my mind and heart. I saw a group of passionate believers in Jesus Christ who loved God, the church and the community. This vision took shape as I began to serve, witness, preach and lead in my new ministry setting. Serving in a life-giving ethos gave me the impetus to see life, the church and ministry differently. It motivated me to use my time to do something with my life that has eternal value. It sustained me in times of darkness.

I still remember a phrase used by Victor Frankl (quoting Nietzsche) from my time in seminary, *"He who has a why can bear any how."* Frankl himself survived the Holocaust and spoke of those who lived through the death camps in World War II. He said that in their suffering, people do not despair when they see some meaning in their lives. That meaning could be the memory of a loved one or an unfinished project. Frankl survived the concentration camp because he remembered that he had to finish a manuscript he had been working on. Fresh vision certainly gave new meaning to my life and caused me to persevere.

This new momentum and motivation inspired me to set the direction and vision for the new church we were planting. In doing so, I was not constrained by a static culture, a central hierarchy or by bureaucracy. I had the freedom to focus the vision and resources of the church on evangelism. This vision had to be translated into reality.

No Longer Pre-programmed

Freedom from a stylised and predetermined system of ministry was a particularly important change for me. I can now be spontaneous and am no longer controlled by an institution and the continuation of its culture and methods. We have a more informal style of worship, play contemporary music and use all kinds of instruments. The members of the congregation can participate by using the gifts of the Holy Spirit and by sharing testimonies or accounts of what God has done in their lives.

I was able to free myself from the constraints of the Church system and let Jesus and his Spirit guide me. This meant being free to pray and prophesy spontaneously. Since the congregation is free to use the gifts of the Holy Spirit, we have experienced many healings, miracles, and conversions. In one service, a man's back was miraculously healed. A woman came out of the waters of Baptism and found that her rejection and fear of people had disappeared. We have seen a baby's brain healed and the mother give birth to a healthy child after brain lesions were discovered in the womb. Numerous people were miraculously delivered from their drug addiction. Others were freed from their debts through debt counselling run by us. One woman had a revelation of a specific and serious heart condition that had not been diagnosed by a consultant.

A gentleman named Keith went to see a top consultant with some symptoms. After tests and an X-ray, Keith was diagnosed with pulmonary fibrosis, which is actually a death sentence. At a follow-up appointment a year later and more x-rays, the consultant informed him he could not find the scar. The consultant was dumb founded and could offer no explanation.

The common thread running through all these deliverances, healings and miracles is openness to the Holy Spirit and the power of persistent prayer.

Facilitator not Mediator

In my role as a pastor, I am a facilitator rather than a mediator. A pastor is set apart only by his or her unique gifts to help people grow in their personal relationship with Jesus Christ.

I learned that to be an empowering leader needs more than a title. As John Maxwell says, *"True leadership cannot be awarded, appointed, or assigned. It comes only from influence, and that cannot be mandated. It must be earned. The only thing a title can buy is a little time – either to increase your level of influence with others or erase it."*[98]

The title of 'Father' gave me prestige but very limited influence to change the culture of the churches in which I served. In my new role, my influence did not come from my title as pastor, my university degrees or previous experience. My influence grew gradually by investing my time and skills in people and in the church. It was the result of a life of integrity and hard work.

---

98 John Maxwell, *The 21 Irrefutable Laws of Leadership* (Springfield, Life Publishers International, 2006), p.14

I found that when you help people and stand by them, they are more willing to rally around you and support you.

Empowering people I found was very empathic. To empower and help others is one of the main reasons we are on this planet. The New Testament makes it clear that God wants us to organise ourselves according to the gifts of our members. This means that we must be willing to organise around passionate and gifted people. As leaders, we help others to realise their dreams and that means empowering them.

My journey has taken me away from a one-man-band style of ministry to teamwork and a mindset that embraces the servant-leader model of ministry. I will never be able to play an effective role in a team if I am a one-man-band player. A loner and an individualist who is only concerned with fulfilling their own potential, will never integrate into a team. They are missing that healing, empathic power of collaboration, and then releasing and helping others.

Rediscovering my Humanity

I certainly boarded a different train when I got married, but it was one of the best things I ever did in life. Instead of living a solitary life of celibacy, separated from society, I lived among the people as a married man and was fully integrated into the community. By giving up my privileged position, I regained the ability to live as a human being among other human beings.

The vocation to serve in a local church is a vocation to live, share, serve and evangelise in the communities to which one belongs. Integration at this level means that it is best to be married for all sorts of moral, spiritual, and practical reasons. There is, of course, the exception of the pastor who has a genuine vocation to live the single life.

Marriage has been the greatest blessing in my life. It is a divine gift and must be honoured, respected, and promoted for all people today. The damage done to marriage in the past by the unbiblical rules and teachings of the Church must be vigorously redressed. The only way to achieve this is to make a tectonic decision to abolish celibacy. This alone would send an unmistakable message that celibacy is not a superior way of life to marriage.

My testimony is that marriage to a wonderful woman has in no way affected my productivity as a preacher of the gospel. The claim that celibacy enables unmarried priests to be more fruitful in ministry does not stand up to scrutiny. Many of Jesus' disciples were married and had children. Yet these men were productive ministers who spread Christianity to far flung parts of the world. When you see the incredible fruitfulness of married couples serving in other denominations today, you must ask yourself, *"How does their love relationship negatively affect their ministry?"* A productive life as a servant of Jesus Christ has nothing to do with marriage or celibacy. It is about lifestyle, leadership, and teamwork where all church members, not just an elite few, are encouraged and empowered to use their God-given talents.

Marriage opens up a multitude of opportunities for service that imposed celibacy does not. Yes, marriage has its *"worldly troubles"*,[99] but celibacy has problems of a different kind. I believe that any problem marriage brings can be overcome if one takes a healthy approach to dealing with it. One does not have to struggle with these difficulties but can overcome them by the grace of God and by learning some valuable communication and conflict resolution skills. As we shall see, the difficulties inherent in enforced celibacy relate to human impulses that cannot be prayed away, and no amount of training can counteract the force of nature. In my experience, the benefits of marriage far

---

99 1 Corinthians 7:28

outweigh the benefits of celibacy. For any person, man or woman, celibacy is never a good choice when God has designed you to *"Be fruitful and increase in number; fill the earth and subdue it."*[100]

Marriage is not perfect, but it promotes more purity and freedom than obligatory celibacy ever could. There is also great freedom in belonging to a church where moral theologians do not feel obliged to comment on issues related to the intimate activities of a married couple in the bedroom. Pentecostalism promotes love and consent in marriage and leaves the details to the individual conscience of the couple. The first time I heard a significant leader say that theologians should stay out of the bedroom was a eureka moment for me.

Governance and Oversight

As a pastor, I am under the authority of a locally governed church made up of elders and church board members, not Rome. This is in keeping with the New Testament way of doing church. The New Testament gives not only examples but also teaching principles for church government.

The Bible clearly teaches that we are to respect and obey those who have temporal authority over us. The Church is not a law unto itself. Many government directives, such as those on child protection, health and safety, in no way contradict what God requires of us, and actually promote godly standards. In contrast to the secrecy and cover-ups of the Catholic Church, it makes sense for a church council with a culture of transparency to oversee the implementation of these sensible regulations.

---

100 Genesis 1:28

Our church is a self-governing organisation that makes its own spiritual, financial, staffing, and administrative decisions. This has huge advantages because it allows us to be creative and keep the momentum going by making quick decisions. We can be innovative and change church structures if that helps the church and people grow.

There are no gender restrictions and women are free to take any position or role in the church. I believe that today's male-dominated churches have their roots in the teaching of St Augustine, but they justify their position with a distorted interpretation of the Bible. Augustine's teaching has a reach far beyond the Catholic Church.[101]

Flourishing

With Paul came a way of working where church members were trained and released into ministry. This letting go of control was a new experience. At the same time there was a system of accountability which is very important in this context of freedom.

Paul's leadership opened a whole new world. He gave me the opportunity to preach, teach and mentor people. Organising and leading a district-wide counselling course was a fantastic opportunity. He put me in charge of all kinds of activities over a period of fourteen years. These activities included having responsibility for small groups and leading mission trips to Africa. Under Paul's leadership I flourished.

I may give the impression that all was rosy in the garden in my relationship with Paul. But that was not always the case. He was not perfect, and neither

---

101 See chapter 16 for more information on Saint Augustine.

was I, but I was not going to let that affect the overall direction of our relationship or derail the vision I had. There are times when we need to cut our leaders some slack. They are not perfect! In any case, God always uses these disappointments to bring about His plan in our lives, in the grand scheme of things.

Being a pastor and leader at heart, I had real vision to lead my own church and working with Paul was great preparation. Desiring to be productive and fruitful for God, I was willing to invest time and toil for this. Imagine a crippled, tired old shrub coming to life, nurtured by its new surroundings to blossom. Something similar happened to me. Andy Rooney, the American journalist, and essayist is quoted as saying, *"Everyone wants to live on top of the mountain, but all the happiness and growth occurs while you're climbing it."*[102] I really enjoyed the journey and finding new ways of doing church. I was able to change and leave behind the tired rituals and routines I had grown up with.

Making course corrections eventually paid dividends. I am no longer in that swirling black hole of intense negative energy that sucks you in, drains you and affects your whole life. By God's grace, I have found a way to free myself from those voices that were pulling me backwards. I feel valued and I have been able to regain my self-respect.

The most important course correction I made was to find an environment for preaching the gospel where there was an expectation that it would be accepted. I had to make sure that I myself had heard and responded to the true gospel. I did not want to preach a false gospel and thereby give people false hope.

---

102 Andy Rooney, https://www.unicothings.com/quotes-on-transition/

CHAPTER 14

WORKING OUT MY SALVATION

"We are saved by grace, through faith in Christ alone! And since there is no room for human merit there can be no grounds for human boasting."[103]

Are They in Heaven?

Is there a difference between the gospel I preach now and the gospel the Catholic Church preaches? Over the past twenty-five years, I preached at many funerals at which members of the family often give a moving eulogy in which they talk about the amazing, good deeds of their deceased relative.

During the message, I ask the question, *"Have they done enough to earn their way into Heaven?"* Most people would say that their lives of love and good deeds certainly qualify them. We value good deeds, but I must tell people that is not why they are saved.

They are in Heaven because they received God's free gift of forgiveness through Jesus, not because they were wonderful human beings. We are saved because Jesus saved us. Jesus' work on the cross, the shedding of His blood is the basis of our confidence. Since it says in the Bible that *"all have sinned*

---

103 Steve Camp

and fall short of the glory of God,"[104] we can only have confidence in Jesus and never in our own good deeds.

The bar for entering God's presence is so high that even the best of us falls way below the standard needed. The problem is that we often set our own bar, rather than looking to God's standards. But the good news is that God made a way for us to achieve His high standards and it had nothing to do with our performance. God made a way where there was no way. He sent Jesus so that anyone who comes to God through Him will be accepted as one who has reached God's high standards. Because you come through Jesus, you now have God's seal of approval on your life.[105] Our confidence is based on what Jesus did, not on what we do.

But What Is the Gospel?

In 1 Corinthians 15, Saint Paul summarises the gospel very briefly. He began by declaring, *"I want to remind you of the gospel I preached to you, which you received and on which you have taken your stand."*[106] Then he went on: *"For what I received I passed on to you as of first importance: that Christ died for our sins according to the Scriptures…"*[107]

"Christ died for our sins" is *"of first importance"* and is the pinnacle of the genuine gospel. This event can never be replicated or repeated in the Mass.

---

104 Romans 3:23

105 2 Corinthians 5:21 ESV, *"For our sake he made him to be sin who knew no sin, so that in him we might become the righteousness of God."*

106 1 Corinthians 15:1

107 1 Corinthians 15:3

The letter to the Hebrews states, *"But when this priest had offered for all time one sacrifice for sins, he sat down at the right hand of God."*[108]

There are many stories about the bond between twins and the sacrifices they make for each other. Jonny and Alistair Brownlee are not only famous sportsmen but also twins. It is clear from their story that they will always support each other

One such incident occurred in Mexico in 2016, during the World Triathlon Series. Jonny was in the lead with 2 km to go. However, he was dazed and suffering from heat stroke. He started meandering across the track and fell down. Alistair, who was running comfortably behind Jonny, came up to him, helped him up and practically carried him and then pushed Jonny across the finish line in front of him. Alistair said his brother's condition was *"as close to death as you can be in sport."* Alistair sacrificed his own chances to win the race to help his brother over the line.

This gives us some idea, however inadequate, of what Jesus did for us. It tells us that He is always there for us. He gave up his place in heaven to help us across the finish line. When we were helpless, when we had sinned and fallen short of God's glory, God sent Jesus to sacrifice himself and share with us a place on the podium that belonged only to Him.

When the gospel is preached today, sin is rarely mentioned. Before we come to know Christ, sin is not the state of being *"as close to spiritual death as possible,"* it is spiritual death. It is the core problem of humanity, and Christ's death on the cross is the answer to it. When Paul arrived in Corinth, he said, *"For I resolved to know nothing while I was with you except Jesus Christ and him crucified."*[109]

---

108 Hebrews 10:12

109 1 Corinthians 2:2

Jonny Brownlee could not make it to the finish line in his own strength. Neither can we. Without Christ, we are spiritually dead, and we are totally incapable of saving ourselves. That is why St Paul decided, at Corinth, to know nothing except Christ and Him crucified. David Pawson sums it up succinctly, *"Christ's finished work on the cross is objectively sufficient, in and of itself, to save the world from sin. Nothing can, much less need, be added to it."*[110] A conscious decision to accept that I am a sinner (spiritually dead) and that my sins have been cleansed by the blood of Jesus is an essential prerequisite for receiving the gospel. Jesus has given me that 'medical' help that is needed to 'resurrect' me.

The second proclamation of Paul's gospel is that Christ was buried. Most preachers seldom mention Christ's burial, but Jesus' burial is as significant as His death or resurrection.[111] The burial was crucial because it proved that Jesus was dead. When something dies, you do not leave it lying around, you bury it. You can call Jesus an extraordinary person if He survived the crucifixion, but that's all. It was necessary that Jesus died, because that was God's purpose for reconciling humanity to Himself.[112]

Finally, in his third statement about the gospel, Paul then speaks about the resurrection.[113] The resurrection is His vindication. It is the capstone of the gospel. If the story ended with His death and burial, there would be no gospel, no forgiveness or eternal life. The words He spoke about His power to forgive sins while alive would all be a lie. But God, in raising Him from

---

110 David Pawson, *The Normal Christian Birth, How to Give New Believers a Proper Start in Life,* (Kindle Edition), p.14

111 1 Corinthians 15:4 *"... that he was buried"*

112 Hebrews 9:26 *"He has appeared once for all at the culmination of the ages to do away with sin by the sacrifice of himself."*

113 1 Corinthians 15:4-5: *"...that he was raised on the third day according to the Scriptures, and that he appeared to Cephas, and then to the Twelve."*

the dead is declaring loud and clear that there is forgiveness of sins in Jesus; there is such a thing as the resurrection of the dead and eternal life for those who die believing in Him.

So, What Is the Difference?

"Is there a difference between the gospel I preach now, and the gospel the Catholic Church preaches?" Catholics and Protestants today work side by side on critical issues such as moral and social issues. You will find many born-again Christians in the Catholic Church. The fact that Protestants and Catholics respect each other is a good thing. However, there are still significant differences, and these differences are not trivial.

I agree with the position that salvation is by faith alone, by grace alone, and in Christ alone. Salvation comes to your soul at a certain point in time when you clearly realise how harmful sin is and how much God hates it. This means that the Holy Spirit is convicting you. This conviction compels you to turn to Christ to receive the comfort of forgiveness which he graciously gives you. Genuine faith is preceded by repentance, which involves a sincere intention to give up a sinful lifestyle. It is not just a matter of 'saying sorry' for one's sins. Salvation is a gift from God, but it is also a conscious decision and a very personal moment. I remember well the moment when the Holy Spirit showed me my sin and I turned to Christ and felt the weight of sin fall off me.

In contrast, the Roman Catholic Church views salvation as a process that does not depend on Christ alone, but is obtained through Baptism, keeping the commandments and taking part in the sacraments. This means that the Church encourages Catholics to continue to strive for salvation.

Today, I do not believe in having to work for salvation, I believe in working it out. Salvation is already given. You work out your salvation by keeping the commandments, doing good deeds inspired by the Holy Spirit and taking part in the life of the church. That is a significant difference, and both cannot be right. One position makes you doubt your salvation and encourages you to keep working for it. The other gives you great assurance that you are already saved and spurs you on to work out your salvation with love and gratitude.

What About Water Baptism?

I was 'christened' as a baby the day after I was born. My Baptism by total immersion in water took place in Jerusalem on 4 July 1981 in a swimming pool in someone's back garden. I consider this 'Believer's Baptism' to be an important part of my conversion experience. However, I would not say it is essential to salvation. The good thief on the cross went to 'paradise' and there was no opportunity to baptise him. When we study the early Church Fathers, we find that they believed that Water Baptism was part of the conversion experience. At the same time, none of them taught that salvation was impossible without Baptism. But it would be a mistake to treat Baptism as an optional extra.

Water Baptism has taken on great significance for me for several reasons. First, it is a symbol that all my sins have been washed away and I am accepted as a child of God. Nevertheless, to view Baptism as purely symbolic is to neglect its powerful life-changing qualities.

Not only have I accepted Christ as my saviour, but through going into the water of Baptism, I have identified myself with Christ who descended into death, and I have died to my old life. In fact, the devil had to give up any claim of ownership over me. In his biography, *Luther: Man Between God and the Devil,* Heiko Oberman quotes Luther: *"The only way to drive away the Devil is through faith in Christ, by saying: 'I have been baptized, I am a Christian.' "*[114] When Luther experienced one of his bouts of depression, he would say *"Baptisatus Sum"* (*"I am baptised"*).

Eric Maddison once told me of an ex-satanist who was baptised by complete immersion in water. He had satanic tattoos on his body, but when he emerged from the water the tattoos had disappeared. The distinctive Roman Catholic mark of ownership on a priest's life is celibacy. I believe that when I came out of the waters of Baptism, that mark was no longer there. The effects of spiritualism and fortune telling were also no longer there. Legally, I was now free from any claim of ownership over my life, apart from the claim of Jesus Christ. I now belonged to Him.

In Baptism there is a real connection, call it 'sacramental', with the grace of God through faith. This grace is not only retroactive, forgiving past sins, but it is also future-oriented for a Christ-like life here on earth. We need to be clear that Baptism does not add to your salvation or make you more acceptable to God. In Baptism and through faith, you experience God's grace for the struggles and challenges that lie ahead as your life is hidden with Christ.

Spiritual warfare is the cosmic war of good against evil. It is a battle between God and Satan which is fought out in every child of God and in every local church. As Saint Paul said, *"our struggle is not against flesh and blood."*[115] As a pastor, I was constantly involved in 'spiritual warfare.'

---

114 https://bredenhof.ca/2017/01/26/luther-baptizatus-sum-i-am-baptized/
115 Ephesians 6:12

CHAPTER 15

SPIRITUAL WARFARE

"For our struggle is not against flesh and blood..."[116]

Martin Luther once said, *"Now when the devil saw that God was building such a holy church, he was not idle and built his chapel beside it, which was greater than God's temple."*[117] This is so true. Marching to the beat of the drum on a road less travelled has the potential for the devil to introduce dissonant and discordant notes and much worse. The devil is not idle if the church is in your bones and if building church is part of your DNA.

There is a character called Diotrephes in the Bible that Saint John writes about: "*I wrote to the church, but Diotrephes, who loves to be first, will not welcome us. So, when I come, I will call attention to what he is doing, spreading malicious nonsense about us.*" [118]

If this character makes an appearance in your church, watch out. He will endanger the peace of the church and spread "*malicious nonsense*" about you. It happened on my watch. His game is to take over and gain authority rather than be available for service. Diotrephes craves dominance and is willing to

---

116 Ephesians 6:12

117 Martin Luther, *Luther's Works* (1517 Media; Fortress Press, 1966), v. 41, p.167-168

118 3 John 1:0-11

do anything to gain it. He does not care how many people get hurt, what lies he spreads or how much chaos his actions cause.

He will carefully infiltrate his way into your community before accusing you of various forms of deceit behind your back. You may be accused of all kinds of fraud including stealing substantial amounts of money. Members will be told to stop donating or leave the church.[119] Diotrephes is toxic and makes up lies that threatened your leadership position. He will contact other leaders and try to persuade them to stand against you.

However, if your church is biblically organised, has good governance and financial safeguards in place, the godly character of your church will not allow a single person leading a small group to hold sway over a discerning congregation. While he may play on the weakness and resentment of some members, the vast majority will stand by you, and you will be able to show him the door.

Diotrephes is only one of many manifestations of the devil as he tries to incorporate God's temple into his chapel.

These targeted attacks by the devil are balanced by the backing of incredible supporters. In my years of ministry, I have met extraordinarily faithful people. Their lives are in harmony with the life of the church. *"Many claim to have unfailing love, but a faithful person who can find?"*[120] In every world, the word 'faithfulness' stands tall. This was so clear when Diotrephes came calling with false accusations a few years ago. Colleagues who knew Liz and me, stood up in the congregation in our absence and expressed their confi-

---

119 Proverbs 6:16 tells us that among the seven things God hates is, *"...a false witness who pours out lies and a person who stirs up conflict in the community."*
120 Proverbs 20:6

dence in us and the way the church was being run. I describe people like this as 'pure gold.'

Colleagues who keep their promises deter our spiritual enemies, and lift morale. These brothers and sisters walk in humility. Paul tells the Ephesians *"to walk in a manner worthy of the calling to which you have been called, with all humility and gentleness."*[121] Humility is the basis of unity because wherever you find pride, you will not find unity. People build reputations and those who walk in pride bring disunity or break away if they do not address their issues.

The people you include in your 'inner circle' will decide your success or failure as a pastor. Therefore, it is important to choose carefully and then nurture and train the people who are closest to you.

Rejection

Rejection is a repressive spirit, and it robbed me of my joy and peace for a long time. It is a tactic of the enemy that prevents you from experiencing freedom and the presence of God's love in your life. This happened to me not only as a priest, but I also experienced it as a pastor.

When you refuse to be controlling, when everyone can rightly hear from God, and when you add to that a mixture of toxic or dysfunctional people, trouble or disappointment is bound to happen. As a senior pastor, you put your heart and soul into serving the church and its members. You feel at one with the vision. Your life is fully interwoven with the church, but the members sometimes have a different perspective. The response is not always

---

121 Ephesians 4:1-2

what you expect. That unexpected response sometimes comes from those who were once friends, leaders, and allies. Those who made promises do not keep them and people let you down. I do not condemn that. I have come to realise that we carry the burden of their 'rejection' because we have invested so much in the vision and because we placed so much trust in them.

Rejection in ministry can be nuclear. These experiences of rejection have always been linked to close and meaningful relationships with people you trust. After all, we are all one family and you do not expect family members to abandon you or abuse you. Just as rejection by a friend can be very painful, wounds inflicted through trusted members of the family of God can be devastating. The most difficult thing is when you walk with people through their difficult times, you give them opportunities for ministry, you support them unconditionally, and then they leave.

We can all learn something from professional sport. On the Lions tour to South Africa in 1997, Jason Leonard was called up to the squad but did not feature in any of the three Test matches. Nevertheless, he was totally committed to ensuring that those who were selected in his place were given the best preparation to win. He supported them to the best of his ability and helped them in training with scrummaging, lineouts, rucking and mauling. What a great attitude!

Professional footballers are taught to be there for each other. Regardless of how they get along with the manager and how long they stay at the club, they are taught to be there when they are playing or not playing, when they are in form or out of form, when they sit on the bench or when they are sent onto the field of play. They are taught to have a good attitude when they are substituted or when they play the full ninety minutes. It is about being there to support others on the team. Many people today, even Christians, do not have that concept. Roy Todd once said, *"Never underestimate the power of just showing up."*[122]

You can prepare yourself for rejection, but you cannot inoculate yourself completely against it. It always hurts when you experience it. It seems our brains are wired to react that way. Every time it happens, a little piece of the dream disappears, no matter how well you arm yourself against it.

It is important to learn from experience and I have some experience of dealing with rejection. The lessons did not all come at once, and I am still learning. Here is what I tend to do in response to these experiences, and you can put some of these ideas into practise too.

Accept rejection rather than wallow in it. This is an act of your will and does not depend on your feelings. Accept it and stop fighting it. You cannot do anything about it unless you have to apologise. Above all, do not succumb to the temptation to criticise yourself and constantly analyse what you did wrong. By all means learn from it, but there is no need to punish yourself. As I said, rejection is often about other people's problems, not your own. It is also true that when I have rejected someone, and I have, it has often been more about me and my insecurities than about the other person.

Forgive and refuse to demonise those who have rejected you. Forgive them and pray for them so that their expectations, even if you could not fulfil them, may be met in their new environment. Try to see them through the lens of love. All this is not easy, but it has helped me to move on.

Find comfort and healing in community, in relationships, in love, in finding new alliances and in mentorship. Strength comes from these

---

122 Roy & Lydia Todd are the pioneers and lead pastors of the Junction Church in Loughborough, Leicester & Nottingham.

relationships, but most of all from your relationship with God. Take direction from reading Ephesians chapter 6.

Use your good qualities to get the dream going again. What you do may be small but use the gifts that brought you success in the past to create forward momentum.

Only tell your story on a need-to-know basis. If you keep telling your story to everyone else, you will hold on to it and that will only increase your negative feelings.

I had to deal with the rejection, shame and repercussions of Church decrees that put a curse on a priest who no longer submits to the rule of celibacy. It was important to shed the aura of demonisation and get rid of this old mindset if I wanted to focus effectively on my new calling.

We all need to analyse our experiences in the light of the Word of God with the help of the Holy Spirit to improve the way we learn, live and work as Christians. Over the years, through reflection, I developed a theology for leaving the priesthood. Reflection and good theology produce good practice, informed actions and better systems. This theology has enabled me to deal with shame and lack of self-respect. It has empowered me to live a life of more obedience and I have gained better closure and greater peace of mind as a result.

CHAPTER 16

ROOTS OF CELIBACY

"Bad theology will eventually hurt people and dishonour God in proportion to its badness."[123]

The Roots of Celibacy

I began by examining the roots of celibacy to find out if they aligned with good practice and biblical principles. If the roots are good, the fruits will also be good and vice versa.

I began to read and study subjects that were never taught in the seminary. I found that the leadership of the Church between AD 300 and AD 400 took some wrong paths. Initially, the angle of error may have been small, but the divergence over the centuries has been great indeed.

This is especially true of the roots of celibacy and attitudes to sex and marriage. I discovered shameful trends. There is an unchristian history of injustice, cruelty, and sexual phobia that underpins the roots of celibacy. I was horrified to discover that sex-hostile attitudes towards women and marriage were clear from early on. These attitudes did not come from Jesus, but from outside the Church. Paganism, Stoicism, Manichaeism, and Gnosticism are the main sources of this false teaching.

---

123 John Piper

Saint Augustine (AD 354-430) played a leading role in opening the door of the Church to hatred of pleasure, women, marriage, and all kinds of enjoyment. Augustine was deeply fixated on sex. In his early years, he loved it, and in his later years he hated and condemned it. He was deeply pained by his past experiences, and it is his negative views about sexuality that predominate. His statement that marriage was only marginally less sinful than fornication, set the pattern for the following centuries.

Augustine went on to be the most influential Christian thinker of his time and arguably of all time. His big guns fired some important salvos in a long history of oppression of priests and women. It was this kind of teaching that began to place celibacy above marriage and eventually led to it becoming compulsory for all clergy.

Augustine's misogyny is shown in his statement that a man loves his wife because she is a human being, but *"hates the fact that she is a woman."*[124] He believed that virginity was superior to marriage and that the sexual act in marriage should not be enjoyed, even if it was for the procreation of children.

The only good that Saint Jerome could find in marriage was that it produced virgins.[125] Saint John Chrysostom wrote, *"As you do, I also think that virginity is a good thing, better than the nuptial life. I add that it is as superior to the nuptial life as Heaven is superior to earth, or as Angels to men."*[126] These men were a disaster for the cause of marriage, and they triggered all kinds of problems for married couples in the centuries that followed. The Church took up the cause of hatred of pleasure and promoted celibacy among the clergy as a superior way of life to marriage.

---

124 Saint Augustine, *Sermon on the Mount*

125 Saint Jerome, *Epistle to Eustochium,* Epistle 22, 20

126 Saint John Chrysostom, *Virginity Is Higher than Matrimony*, p.1

Augustine then developed his own doctrine, which was to have a profound influence on the history of the Church – the doctrine of original sin. He was the first thinker to use this term. This doctrine states that we were all conceived in depravity because of the sin of Adam and Eve. This depravity was passed on to all humanity. For Augustine, the means of passing on original sin was the pleasure a couple had during sexual intercourse. Certainly, marriage *"was stigmatised as the means of transmitting and perpetuating original sin"* in the writings of the Fathers.[127] This led to all kinds of anxieties about sex in the minds of married couples. This teaching turned what should have been a natural, joyful, God-given gift into an anxiety laden guilt trip when a married couple had sex.

We may not agree with Augustine today, but his teaching was the spark that gave rise to an entire system of male, celibate priests. It was responsible for the devaluation of marriage and produced a system of moral theology obsessed with sex.

Since the Church is involved in a battle with evil, and sex is considered evil, the Church felt compelled to take a stand on all issues related to sex. It is therefore not surprising that moral theologians over the centuries became incredibly involved in the private affairs of the bedroom. This is logical, but a big mistake. Theologians have dealt with all sorts of sexual questions. Questions like 'Is disability caused by sex during menstruation? At what point does sex for procreation become sinful? Should menstruating women be allowed to take Communion? Is sex with a menstruating woman a mortal sin or a venial sin? Is sex with a beautiful woman more or less sinful?' Celibate male

---

127 Henry C Lea, *An Historical Sketch of Sacerdotal Celibacy in the Christian Church (Kindle)*, p.30

theologians even felt qualified to judge morally acceptable positions for the sexual act.

In the centuries after Augustine the Church hierarchy resorted to criminal activities and shameful tactics to force the clergy into a compulsory unmarried state. These included selling priests' wives into slavery,[128] and women who had previously made a positive contribution to the work of the Church were now sex-shamed and exposed to a variety of vulgarities. Peter Damian, who died in 1072, referred to them as *"whores, prostitutes... impure spirits, demi-goddesses, sirens, witches"*[129] and other insulting names. Other tactics involved selling the children of priests into slavery and abandoning the clergy to the streets without a livelihood. Priests were imprisoned, whipped, and threatened with eternal damnation. The Church separated spouses and dissolved legal marriages, which the Church had no authority to do. Bishops who did not implement the law were excommunicated. The Council of Trent imposed a curse on any ordained cleric who refused to ask God for the gift of celibacy.

The Catholic Church used all its papal power to penalise priests who refused the practice. All this was very dishonourable. With such unjust and inhumane methods, they sought to inflict their will on priests. Eventually the pope prevailed, and celibacy was imposed on all clergy in 1123 and again in 1139. One could not in a million years claim that the Holy Spirit sanctioned these disgraceful and unbiblical practices.

These crimes occurred against the backdrop of a collapsed society in Europe. The Church entered this vacuum and became so powerful that no

---

128 Henry C Lea, *An Historical Sketch of Sacerdotal Celibacy in the Christian Church*, p.194

129 Peter Ellis Berresford, *Celibacy in the Catholic Church*, https://www.archive.irishdemocrat.co.uk/features/celibacy-in-the-church/

one could challenge it. The Church ruled not just the spiritual realm but the political as well. Henry C. Lea aptly describes how the pope dictated to the whole of Europe from his pontifical throne and the *"humble minister of the altar"* exercised no less power at the local level.[130]

Therefore, there is no justification today for approving the spiritual and secular edifice erected on the basis of false doctrines, appalling attitudes and unchristian actions. The Holy Spirit blows where He wills, and He has no problem blowing on the lives of individual Catholics, nor on the lives of many individual God-fearing priests and lay people who are doing great work. At the same time, I cannot see the Holy Spirit approving of a system built on the foundation of injustice. How can anything good come out of it when families are divided in such a hostile and aggressive way?

A System That Promotes Immorality

In my inner search for a theology of leaving, the second area I examined was the positive or negative effect of celibacy on the morals of the clergy. A practice that is not morally or ethically sound cannot be humanly or theologically correct.

When celibacy was introduced in the twelfth century, immorality was rife among the clergy. Church reformers of the time believed that celibacy, if imposed on the clergy, would solve this major problem, and promote holiness of life. However, the belief that the imposition of celibacy and excessive

---

130 Henry C Lea, *An Historical Sketch of Sacerdotal Celibacy in the Christian Church*, p.6

161

self-denial would solve the problem of immorality was a mistake. A secular church diagnosed the problem but applied the wrong remedy.

A.W. Richard Sipe, a researcher, psychotherapist, and former priest, interviewed many priests about their sexual practices. He found that at any given time, fifty percent of the priests were celibate. This means that fifty percent are not. He found that thirty percent are in opposite-sex and fifteen percent are in same-sex relationships. Six percent are engaged with minors. If this is a snapshot at a point in time, the reality must be that many more priests have problems with celibacy at some point in their lives. Sipe claims that just 2 percent of priests achieve the aim of remaining celibate throughout their lives. His findings are based on actual counts of the sexual practices of one thousand five hundred priests.[131]

The iron law of celibacy denies intimacy to the clergy, which in turn creates a pressure-cooker situation that needs release. Unfortunately, this release usually manifests itself in secret sins and immorality. Statistics show that celibacy does not lead priests to greater devotion to their flock, but to clandestine affairs and it drives them into sin rather than greater purity. Priests find refuge not only in sexual sins but also in many other forms of transgression.

If celibacy were proposed to Saint Paul as a solution to immorality, he would say that the law has no power to change us or make us holy. It does not free us from immorality, for the purpose of the law is simply to make us aware of sin.[132] The law of celibacy or any other law for that matter, has no power to enable any priest to live a holy life or to avoid immorality.

---

131 A.W. Richard Sipe, *Celibacy, A Secret World,* (Kindle), Location 54
132 Romans 7:7–8

We know from American history that the Prohibition Act did not prevent drinking. In many ways, it made drinking more attractive to people because of our desire to break boundaries set by the law. When someone draws a boundary for us, we are at once tempted to cross that line. Regarding celibacy, it is prevention that fuels a priest's desire for intimacy. This is not the fault of the law. It is the fault of our sinful hearts. So, what priests need is not a law, but a new heart in order to deal with immorality.

Christ alone can conquer sin, not the law of celibacy. When I received a new heart from God through faith in Jesus, I allowed Christ to take control of my life and I found that it was *"for freedom that Christ had set us free."*[133] This is the key. Once we receive a new heart, we are free from the bondage of sin. The Holy Spirit can lead you into marriage or He can also guide you into celibacy, and for those who are celibate at heart, it is a free choice and not an imposed law.

If we put ourselves under any law again, we return to our old nature which tempts us to sin. Only Jesus Christ, through the Holy Spirit and a life of faith, can free us from everything that the law of Moses or the law of celibacy cannot free us from. Paul underscores this point for us in Romans, *"For what the Law could not do, weak as it was through the flesh, God did: sending His own Son in the likeness of sinful flesh and as an offering for sin, He condemned sin in the flesh"*.[134]

The evidence shows that celibacy does not promote holiness, but immorality. The whole scenario is a bad business and if the running of the Church could be compared to a war, you could argue that *"There hasn't been a war*

---

133 Galatians 5:1

134 Romans 8:3

run this badly since Olaf the hairy, King of all the Vikings, ordered 80,000 battle helmets with the horns on the inside."[135]

The Church had lost sight of the true gospel of God's power to free us from the bondage of sin. The new so-called gospel was based on what you did for Christ instead of what Christ did for you in condemning sin in the flesh. As this false gospel developed and the church adopted an anti-sex stance, salvation became increasingly about what people did with their genitals, rather than salvation being a gracious gift from God. Relationships between the sexes became the true touchstone for religious devotion.

The shameful history and practices I discovered reinforced my conviction that bad theology leads to bad practice. When shame resurfaces, when I am tempted to give in to lack of self-esteem or guilt, I comfort myself with the answers I found and remind myself that bad theology leads to bad practice. My sanity and self-esteem are bolstered as I find reassurance in good theology.

My search for a theology of leaving, led me to explore another important question. If celibacy is not a helpful or wise practice, what other reasons might there be for introducing it?

---

135 Rowan Atkinson, *Blackadder Goes Forth* (https://inews.co.uk/culture/television/blackadder-quotes-161437)

CHAPTER 17:

THE REAL REASON FOR CELIBACY

*"The Spirit clearly says that in later times some will abandon the faith
and follow deceiving spirits and things taught by demons...
They forbid people to marry...."*[136]

What is the real reason for celibacy in the Catholic Church? The Church says that celibacy is to better imitate the chaste behaviour of Jesus Christ. The evidence clearly shows that this does not happen. While the reform movement of the Cluniac monks, which began in the late 10th century, advocated celibacy for clerics, there were other, more secular reasons for clerical celibacy.

The Church wanted to promote its policy of economic self-preservation. The Church was desperate to protect the ownership of its property and to stop the drain on its financial and economic resources. The easiest way to achieve this was to separate the priests from their families. The Church would prevent them from having legitimate children and separate the priests from their wives. If this plan worked, the priests would have no heirs. This would prevent Church land from being taken out of the possession of the Church.

---

136 1 Timothy 4:1-3

The abusive encounter I had with the cleric before leaving, opened my eyes to what the Catholic Church is all about at its core: control and domination! Considering that the apple does not fall far from the tree, it is not at all surprising that many clerics have a spirit of control, ownership and entitlement. I say "*many*" because it does not apply to all.

A Controlling Superpower

The Catholic Church is often seen as a superpower. Its contribution is crucial to solving global problems. It has the power to flex its muscles on the world stage. When the pope speaks, he at once makes the headlines. Because of its global influence, we can easily ignore the Church's false systems. We cannot ignore a system that promotes control and domination and falsifies the teachings of Jesus and the Bible in general. The reality is that the emperor has no clothes.[137]

Pope Gregory VII (AD 1025–1085), who is called the father of Roman Catholicism, set out the art of control par excellence. When he was appointed pope, he drew up a Dictatus in which he said, among other things, that the pope is above human judgement.[138] As Bishop of Rome, he made all bishops swear an oath of allegiance to him. This meant that the bishops were bishops "*by the favour of the Apostolic See.*" The bishops lost their independence and relinquished control to the papacy, so that the pope was the actual bishop in each diocese. He took complete control of local churches.

---

137 Hans Christian Andersen, *The Emperor's New Clothes*

138 Ernest F. Henderson (translator), *Select Historical Documents of the Middle Ages*, (London: George Bell and Sons, 1910), pp. 366-367

Pope Gregory was not content to have spiritual control, for him the whole earth also belonged to him. In his Dictatus, he claimed the power to depose emperors. He wanted to show that he also controlled the secular realm by forcing Emperor Henry IV to walk barefoot through the snow for days and then grovel before him in the freezing cold at Canossa, clad only in a hair shirt. Gregory abused the spiritual weapon of excommunication against Henry to punish him for his resistance to the power of the Church and to assert political control. Peter De Rosa, another ex-priest, writes: *"In a parody of the gospels, the devil took him up to a very high mountain and showed him all the kingdoms of the world, and Gregory VII licked his lips and cried: These are all mine."*[139]

Gregory, the first pope to force a secular power to submit to him, set the norm and the highest values of the Catholic Church – control and power. Throughout history, the introduction of compulsory celibacy, the 'ontological' nature of the priesthood, the Inquisition, the Crusades, the Counter-Reformation, Papal Infallibility, the doctrine of transubstantiation, and confessing your sins to a priest, have all been about securing and keeping power and control.

Celibacy – A Method of Control

While the ontological nature of the priesthood holds a priest to the Church, the main method of control is celibacy. The promise of celibacy made before a bishop binds a priest to the Church, and celibacy is at the heart of a world

---

139 Peter De Rosa, *Vicars of Christ, The Dark Side of the Papacy* (Kindle), Location 1641

of control and secrecy. The Church controls not only the priests but also the laity. The only way to be in a position of authority in the Church is to be a celibate priest. A layperson, even a priest who has returned to the lay state, cannot hold an official office that signifies authority. Celibacy is about money and control.

Peter De Rosa points out that the celibate priest is the property of the institution: "*A celibate priest owed total allegiance not to wife and children but to the institution. He was the creature of the institution. The Roman system was absolutist and hierarchical. For such a system to work, it needed operatives completely at the beck and call of superiors … The papal system would collapse without the unqualified allegiance of the clergy; celibacy alone could guarantee that sort of allegiance.*"[140]

Going on my personal experience, I agree with De Rosa's assessment. Through a celibate clergy, the Church controls its wealth and keeps absolute control within a small male circle. The male priesthood is the workforce that implements the broken systems and promotes the distorted teachings of the Church.

In my day, the Catholic Church invited conscientious young men with good motives into a system where they became part of the Church's control mechanism. Many men become priests because they believe they are called to the priesthood. When I took a promise of celibacy with little life experience, it was not because I had a gift from God. I made it because in my idealism and immaturity I did not pay enough attention to the wisdom of God's Word and was too willing to listen to the propaganda of the Church.

I hastened to that gift with the papal assurance that God's grace would be sufficient for me. Papal assurance is not adequate when the institution to

---

140 Peter De Rosa, *Vicars of Christ, The Dark Side of the Papacy*, Location 10349

which you belong decides to work outside the framework of God's Word, acting in its own self-interest and control of its assets. In fact, you are opening yourself to deceiving spirits and the Catholic Church is inviting you into a huge struggle. The rule of obligatory celibacy has a veneer of holiness but is in fact a doctrine of demons.[141] I echo the words of Martin Luther in saying that Satan invented compulsory celibacy and it is a fruitful source of sin and wrongdoing.

The Bible clearly sets out the qualifications of a leader in the church in the following passage: "*A bishop (elder) then must be blameless, the husband of one wife, temperate, sober-minded, of good behaviour, hospitable, able to teach.*"[142]

I am now fully convinced that a church leader should be a married man simply because he is better prepared to understand and deal with the many problems that arise in family life. Any authority that is not well exemplified in a family environment should be ruled out of the question. St Paul's view was simple and to the point, "*If anyone does not know how to manage his own family, how can he take care of God's church?*"[143] From this, it is obvious that family life, not seminary education and certainly not imposed celibacy, is the primary proving ground for leadership in the church.

---

141 1 Timothy 4:1
142 1 Timothy 3:2
143 1 Timothy 3:5

Clericalism and the Priesthood

The Bible speaks of *"a holy priesthood"*[144] of all believers. There is no valid reason for a separate elite squad of celibate male clergy other than the desire of the superiors to control everything. The truth is that there is no such thing as 'ordination' in the New Testament which puts an unmistakable priestly imprint on one's character. Saint Paul *"appointed"*[145] elders. He did not ordain them.

Because of their relationship with Christ, all believers have direct access to God, and every Christian can now be called a priest and has no need to submit to the control of a clerical elite. Saint Paul tells Timothy, *"For there is one God and one mediator between God and mankind, the man Christ Jesus, who gave himself as a ransom for all people."*[146]

Priests are there to offer sacrifices, and apart from the sacrifices of obedience, praise and worship, today's 'priests' have nothing to offer. The model of the Old Testament priesthood is redundant. Jesus replaced it by sacrificing himself. There is no need of another intermediary, such as a priest, to control our relationship with God. No human being can stand in our place. Every soul stands for itself in a personal relationship with God.

The doctrine of 'Apostolic Succession' which is believed to transmit spiritual power by the 'laying on of hands' from one generation of clergy to the next, thus ensuring continuation of control, does not stack up. Most scholars, including Catholic ones, think that the Church of Rome was led by

---

144 1 Peter 2:5

145 Acts 14:23

146 1 Timothy 2:5-6

a college of presbyters until well into the second century. There is no evidence for the existence of a presiding bishop or 'pope' in the first century.[147]

Hans Kung, a well-known Catholic theologian, says that while it is accepted that Peter was martyred in Rome, this does not mean that he ever led the church there.[148] Again, Hans Kung says, "*It is historically impossible to find in the initial phase of Christianity an unbroken chain of 'laying on of hands' from the apostles to the present-day bishops.*"[149] Neither the Bible nor history supports the claim of Roman papal authority over priests or bishops.

Henry Chadwick, the distinguished professor at both Oxford and Cambridge, says that there was no call for "*a sustained justification*" of the priority of Roman leadership over the Church before the third century.[150] In fact, there are only sparse references to papal primacy in Church tradition until the eighth century.[151]

The Church does have great power and authority. It is not power to exert domination over people to protect itself. The Church was not put in a privileged position by Jesus to exercise control and entitlement for its own benefit. Jesus was never about controlling people or his leaders. He was about releasing them to preach the Kingdom, to heal the sick, work miracles and to take control over the demonic world. Mark's Gospel says, "*Calling the Twelve to him, he began to send them out two by two and gave them authority over*

---

147 F.A Sullivan, *From Apostles to bishops: the development of the episcopacy in the early church* (New Jersey, Paulist Press International, 2001), p.15

148 Hans Kung, *The Catholic Church: A Short History* (Universal History, Kindle, 2006), p.22

149 Hans Kung, *The Catholic Church, A Short History*, p.31

150 Henry Chadwick, *The Early Church* (Penguin Books, Revised Edition, 1993), p.237

151 Hans King, *Infallible?* (William Collins & Co Ltd, London, 1971), p.91

impure spirits."[152] The seventy-two disciples came back and said they had seen "*Satan fall like lightening from heaven.*"[153] Jesus has given the Church power and authority in the spiritual realm and reserves the exercise of temporal power to Himself when He comes back again. There is never a mention in the Bible texts to say Jesus would give his disciples any worldly power. The task of the Church is to equip and release its ministers for spiritual service.

To combine celibacy and ministry in an unhappy marriage is an abuse of church power. It is a spiritual red herring that distracts the Church from its real purpose which is to engage in spiritual warfare and take control of an evil devilish empire wherever it manifests.

I got into a real dilemma when I submitted to the law of celibacy. It placed me, as Blackadder would say, *"in the stickiest situation since Sticky the stick insect got stuck on a sticky bun."*[154] In quoting Blackadder, I do not want to trivialise my situation, for this is the point where my inner journey towards a theology of leaving becomes very personal. As a 'born-again Christian,' I found myself in a dichotomy between the clear guidance of the Word of God and the demands of the heretical asceticism (self-denial) demanded by the Church. The law of the Church told me that I could not be married, have lifelong companionship or father children. The Word of God said I should not follow deceiving spirits and deny myself the right to a believing wife.[155] Ultimately, there would be only one outcome for me in this struggle.

In the next chapter I will show how I resolved this dilemma and how my frame of mind was helped by a particular understanding of Water Baptism.

---

152 Mark 6:7

153 Luke10:18

154 Rowan Atkinson, *Blackadder Goes Forth,* (www.blackadderquotes.com)

155 1 Corinthians 9:5

My perspective was enhanced by better insight into the Scriptures, the fact that I followed my conscience (inner voice) and relied on a principle grounded in Catholic moral theology. But ultimately The river of healing flows from God's presence in the place of worship.[156]

---

156 Ezekiel 47:12

CHAPTER 18

CLOSURE

"To save the Church, Catholics must detach themselves from the clerical hierarchy—and take the faith back into their own hands."[157]

Paul said to the Romans that any law has power over a person only if they are alive.[158] Paul uses the word *"law"* here in a broad sense, not just the ten commandments, so it could refer to any law, including the law of celibacy. Paul makes it clear that death ends all human contracts related to the law.

Dying to an Unbiblical Contract

I believe that I legally died to Catholicism and its unbiblical systems when I was baptised by full immersion in water in the summer of 1981. At that moment I fully identified myself with the ownership of Christ alone. I was buried in the water of Baptism; I died and was buried with Christ.[159] Every sin and particularly every unbiblical promise was now hidden with Christ in God. I believe that the Catholic Church had to surrender its spiritual and

---

157 James Carrol, *Abolish the Priesthood,* (The Atlantic, June 2019 Issue)

158 Romans 7:1, *"Or do you not know, brethren (for I am speaking to those who know the law), that the law has jurisdiction over a person as long as he lives"*

159 Romans 6:4

legal ownership of me. However, this still had to be worked out in practical terms. I lived in the reality of my old self for two more years until I finally took down the banner of Rome.[160]

Having "*died*" to the ownership of the Church through Baptism, I was now free to belong exclusively to Jesus and to be guided by his Spirit. Under the sole dominion of Jesus, I was free to be led into marriage if the Holy Spirit so led me. Thus, I resolved my dilemma and came fully under the administration of God's Word, where marriage is a God-given right which cannot be set aside by any ecclesiastical regulation.

Legal and Experiential Ownership

Water Baptism gave me the assurance that Jesus is my rightful and legal owner, but I still had to renew in myself a healthy frame of mind and live experientially under His ownership. In the first instance, I was helped in this by a better understanding of the Scriptures.

The Church often invokes the passage in Matthew 19:12[161] as a proof text that Jesus required clergy to be celibate "*for the sake of the Kingdom of Heaven.*" The context of this passage shows that it has nothing to do with celibacy, but that it is about the rejection of adultery, and, by extension, it is about marriage and divorce. Nor is there anything else in Scripture that prescribes celibacy as a criterion for entering the ministry.

---

160 Read Romans 6:1-7

161 "*For there are eunuchs who were born that way, and there are eunuchs who have been made eunuchs by others—and there are those who choose to live like eunuchs for the sake of the kingdom of heaven. The one who can accept this should accept it.*"

There is a hint of asceticism in Paul's writings but no preponderance of scripture that would give a clear picture that celibacy should be linked to ministry. Many people today, not necessarily clerics, still make life difficult and put enormous pressure on themselves to sacrifice marriage and having children in the pursuit of loving God. All Christian service requires sacrifice. This is true but let us be guided by the truth as found in the words of Jesus and the teachings of Holy Scripture. Do not be influenced by zealous practices that have their origins in paganism.

The hardest thing was to let go of the belief that God requires this level of sacrifice in order to show that I was truly devoted to Him. I began to shake off the feeling that I would be disobeying God if I married when I realised that the Scriptures did not require me to be celibate. From this I concluded that the Church should not require this either and that a promise made in addition to the Scriptures and the teachings of Jesus is not binding.

Celibacy is a law that is outside the mandate Jesus gave to the Church. The hierarchy does not have the authority to impose celibacy on a priest. It has no more power to impose celibacy than it has to tell you where to live, who to marry or what career to follow. These are life defining issues about which the Church should be offering support and biblical guidance, not obligations. They should not become life controlling issues. Martin Luther rightly said, *"...the pope has as little power to give this command (to be celibate) as he has to forbid eating, drinking, and the natural process of bodily elimination, or becoming fat."*[162]

Furthermore, Catholic theology teaches that a Christian should not let the threat of excommunication prevent him or her from following his or

---

162 Martin Luther, *An Open Letter to The Christian Nobility*, (Project Wittenberg), https://christian.net/pub/resources/text/wittenberg/luther/web/nblty-05.html, Part 1, no.14

her conscience.[163] As my inner voice was increasingly shaped by a relationship with Jesus and his Word, I followed it because this was the only way to discover my true self.

In Catholic moral theology there is also a principle called *Lex dubia non obligat*. This means that a doubtful or bad law is not obligatory. The law on celibacy is undoubtedly a bad law for the reasons mentioned, and a dissenting priest is not obliged to submit to it.

All this was very reassuring and helped me to renew my thinking so that I could serve Jesus better. However, peace and understanding are found first and foremost in God's presence. The river of healing and freedom flows from the place of worship. Over time, things begin to make sense. In Psalm 73, the psalmist was plagued daily with afflictions. He could find neither peace nor understanding for his situation and was deeply troubled. Only when he entered the sanctuary, the place of worship, did he finally find insight into the fate of his enemies. The best therapy is to sit under God's Word and become still in His presence.

Jesus Has the Final Word

Life under the law of celibacy brought only stress and pressure because the Church imposed an obligation that human nature is unable to bear. Those in the legalist tradition would say, *"Get over it and live with it."* They ignore the words of Jesus who said: *"You're hopeless, you religion scholars! You load*

---

163 Hans King, *Infallible*, p.39

people down with rules and regulations, nearly breaking their backs, but never lift even a finger to help."[164]

Jesus never saw the single life as a necessary condition for ministry. Celibacy, according to Jesus, was only possible for those with the temperament and personality to bear it. He knew there were those who would struggle with the burden of the single life. He cautioned the Scribes and Pharisees against imposing obligations on those who would struggle under the strain. If there is one burden that men will struggle with above anything else, it is the ban on marriage. According to Henry C. Lea, *"He (Jesus) was far indeed from seeking to render obligatory, or even to recommend, practices which only the fervour of fanaticism could render endurable. No teacher before him had ventured to form so lofty a conception of the marriage-tie. It was an institution of God himself whereby man and wife became one flesh."*[165]

Summing Up

The shameful history and practices I discovered reinforced my conviction that bad theology leads to wrong thinking, poor practice and weak discipleship. In this case, bad theology leads to immorality that undermines the integrity and credibility of the Church..

The inhumane and unjust roots of celibacy and the fact that it does not lead to holiness of the clergy are reasons enough to conclude that it is not a good practise. This led me to a very important conclusion. I can better live

---

164 Luke 11:46

165 Henry C. Lea, *An Historical Sketch of Sacerdotal Celibacy in the Christian Church*, p.13

a life of freedom and obedience in the married state. I came to this conclusion because of my studies, a good understanding of the Bible and divine principles.

My testimony is that since I submitted to the conviction of the Word of God and the guidance of the Holy Spirit who led me to switch trains, I am able to live a life of greater stability, obedience and assurance in ministry. Holding on to the bad law of celibacy, living with ungodly compromises and false teachings is detrimental to emotional and spiritual wellbeing and is not worth a brass farthing.

CHAPTER 19

CONCLUSION

"It was the best of times, it was the worst of times"[166]

God rebuilt what was broken and planted anew what was desolate. He did this for the sake of his own name, to save lives. He did it in his own way so that we would have no cause for human boasting. Just as God spoke to the withered bones of the house of Israel in captivity, so he spoke and breathed new life into the embryonic calling that had been in me since childhood and brought it to life. God transformed a barren field of shame and low self-esteem into a flourishing garden.

I can identify to some extent with the story of Joseph in the book of Genesis. It is a remarkable story of someone who was elevated from outcast to prince. Looking back, Joseph could say to his brothers who had sold him as a slave, *"And now, do not be distressed and do not be angry with yourselves for selling me here, because it was to save lives that God sent me ahead of you … So then, it was not you who sent me here, but God."*[167] It seemed as if human involvement had sent me into a desolate wasteland, but in reality it was God. He went ahead of me and prepared a ministry for me that would affect the lives of many people.

---

166 Charles Dickens, *A Tale of Two Cities*.
167 Genesis 45:5,8

Despite the pain that the Catholic Church caused, I would like to thank God for the positive influence it also had on me. As Shakespeare said, *"It was the best of times, it was the worst of times, it was the age of wisdom, it was the age of foolishness, it was the epoch of belief, it was the epoch of incredulity, it was the season of light, it was the season of darkness, it was the spring of hope, it was the winter of despair ..."*

I am very thankful for the two people God chose to raise me. They taught me to fear God and imparted great values to me. The education I received in Church schools and institutions gave me a great start. Leading a disciplined life, having a positive attitude, and living moderately are legacies from my time in the Church. I am grateful for the people in the missionary society I belonged to (Society of African Missions) who contributed greatly to my life and development. I had the great privilege that the Church accepted me for ordination, that people held me in high esteem and took me into their hearts.

However, my overriding feeling today is akin to that of Saint Paul who said, *"What is more, I consider everything a loss because of the surpassing worth of knowing Christ Jesus my Lord, for whose sake I have lost all things. I consider them garbage, that I may gain Christ."*[168]

Now, in the last phase of my life, I am so pleased that my salvation does not depend on my performance. It defies logic that the King of kings, who is so vast that He holds the universe in His hand, sent His Son to befriend you and me. We who have wronged Him and sinned against Him are welcomed into His family and we are saved by grace alone.

---

168 Philippians 3:8

Final Thoughts

One of the greatest joys is to plant a seed and then see the wonder that the seed produces. This journey from seed to miracle is not always exciting and glittering. The seed is buried in the pitch-black earth. Then it is cracked open before the life within it begins the struggle to reach upwards to find light. Only when it finds light does it begin to sprout and continue its journey to become the miracle God intended.

Everything in my life began as a seed. I was given seeds, not silver spoons. Everything had a small beginning, especially the gifts God gave me and my ministry calling. It all started as small seeds that needed the right encouragement and stimulation. My life is a story of the seed breaking open before the life was released. The journey of reaching for the light of truth began before the plan and purpose of God for my life was finally realised.

I would say take seriously the ideas that arise within as everything begins with an idea. Explore that idea carefully and reach upwards to find light. If it seems right to you and the Holy Spirit, dare to step into the unknown and take the leap of faith into God's amazing provision.

At the beginning of this book I said that on the day of my ordination I never thought I would write a book about my break with the Catholic Church. It must also be said that I never imagined that I would lead the kind of life I lead now. Many of the seeds I was given have blossomed into miracles. I am married and still in ministry. I am content, peaceful, but still a work in progress with a long way to go.

Now it is time to move on to the next season. This will not be a season to drop everything, do gardening or sit by a pool. It may be a season to slow down, but it is not a time to abandon the mission to see lives changed. Maybe I will get involved in planting another church! Maybe I will write more books, including a more detailed paper on *"Celibacy and the Roots of the Catholic Church."*

BIBLIOGRAPHY

BOOKS

Walter M. Abbott (General Editor), *The Documents of Vatican II* (London, Geoffrey Chapman, 1967)

David Allen, *The Unfailing Stream, A Charismatic Church History in Outline* (Tonbridge, Sovereign World, 1994)

Don Basham, *A Handbook on the Holy Spirit* (New Kensington, Whitaker House, 1969)

Bartholomew F. Brewer with Alfred W. Furrell, *Pilgrimage from Rome* (Greenville, Bob Jones University Press, 1982)

Catechism Of the Catholic Church Second Edition

Henry Chadwick, *The Early Church* (Penguin Books, Revised Edition, 1993)

James C. Collins and Jerry I. Porras, *Built to Last*, (Collins Business Essentials, An Imprint of HarperCollins Publishers Inc. New York, 1994)

James C. Collins, *From Good to Great* (London, Random House Business, 2001)

Stephen Covey, *The Seven Habits of Highly Effective People* (London, Simon & Schuster, 1989)

Alice Curtayne, *Lough Derg, St. Patrick's Purgatory* (Monaghan, R&S Printers, 1968)

James Dunn, *Baptism in the Holy Spirit* (London, SCM Press, 1970)

Timothy Egan, *The Catholic Church Is Sick with Sex* (New York Times, 31 August 2018)

Raymond Fung, *The Isaiah Vision, An Ecumenical Strategy for Congregational Evangelism* (Geneva, WCC Publications, 1992)

Kevin Gerald, *The Proving Ground, The Nine Tests that Prove Your Personal Potential* (Tulsa, Oklahoma, Insight Publishing Group, 2003)

Wayne Gruden, *Systematic Theology, An Introduction to Biblical Doctrine* (Nottingham, Inter-Varsity Press, 1994)

Ted Honderich, *The Oxford Companion to Philosophy* (Oxford, Oxford University Press, 1995)

Napoleon Hill, *Think and Grow Rich* (Kindle Edition)

Hans King, *Infallible?* (William Collins & Co Ltd, London, 1971)

Deborah Layton, *Seductive Poison: A Jonestown Survivor's Story of Life and Death in the Peoples Temple* (Palatine, Anchor Books, 1999)

Sir John Low, *CAF Giving Index 2018*

Des MacHale (Editor), *Wittypedia, Over 4,000 of the Funniest Quotations* (London, Prion, 2011)

Eric C. Maddison, *Are You Missing God's Best?* (Chichester, New Wine Press, 2004)

Brennan Manning, *The Ragamuffin Gospel, Embracing the Unconditional Love of God* (London, Authentic Media, 2001)

Brennan Manning, *A Stranger to Self-Hatred* (Denville, New Jersey, Dimension Books Inc., 1982)

John C. Maxwell, *Developing the Leaders Around You, How to Help Others Reach Their Potential* (Nashville, Thomas Nelson Publishers, 1995)

John C. Maxwell, *The 21 Indispensable Qualities of a Leader* (Nashville, Thomas Nelson Publishers, 1999)

John C. Maxwell, *The 21 Irrefutable Laws of Leadership* (Springfield, Life Publishers International, 2006)

L. Grant McClung Jr (Editor), *Azusa Street and Beyond* (Lagos, Bridge Publishing, 1986)

Alister E McGrath (Editor), *The Christian Theology Reader* (Oxford, Blackwell Publishing, 1996)

Sean McMahon, *A short History of Ireland* (Dublin, Mercier Press 1996)

Jurgen Moltmann, *The Gospel of Liberation* (Waco, Word Books, 1973)

Beth Moore, *When Godly People Do Ungodly Things* (Nashville, B&H Publishing Group, 2002)

David Petts, *Body Builders. Gifts to make God's People Grow* (Mattersey Hall, 2002)

Karl Rahner, *Meditations on Priestly Life* (London, Sheed, and Ward, 1973)

Thom S Rainer and Eric Geiger, *Simple Church* (Nashville, B&H Publishing Group, 2011)

Uta Ranke-Heinemann, *Eunuchs for the Kingdom of Heaven* (New York, Doubleday, 1990)

Paul Scanlon, *Crossing Over* (Tonbridge, Sovereign World, 2002)

David L. Schindler, *Heart of the World, Center of the Church, Communio Ecclesiology, Liberalism, and Liberation* (Grand Rapids, Eerdmans, 1996)

Ned Sherrin, *The Oxford Dictionary of Humorous Quotations* (Oxford, Oxford University Press, 1995)

A. W. Richard Sipe, *A Secret World: Sexuality and The Search for Celibacy* (London, Psychology Press, 1990)

Graham N Stanton, *Jesus of Nazareth in New Testament Preaching* (Cambridge, Cambridge University Press, 1977)

Cardinal Leo Joseph Suenens, and Dom Helder Camara, *Charismatic Renewal and Social Action. A Dialogue* (London, Darton, Longman and Todd, 1980)

Francis A Sullivan, *From Apostles to bishops: the development of the episcopacy in the early church* (New Jersey, Paulist Press International, 2001)

J.R.R. Tolkien, *Lord of The Rings Trilogy, The Fellowship of the Ring* (London, HarperCollins, 1995)

Max Turner, *The Holy Spirit and Spiritual Gifts Then and Now* (Carlisle, Paternoster Press, 1996)

Max Turner, *Power from on High, The Spirit in Israel's Restoration and Witness in Luke-Acts* (Sheffield, Sheffield Academic Press, 1996)

Max Turner, *Baptism in the Holy Spirit* (Cambridge, Grove Books Ltd, 2000)

Rick Warren, *The Purpose Driven Church* (Grand Rapids, Zondervan Publishing House, 1995)

Philip Yancey, *Grace Notes, Daily readings with a Fellow Pilgrim* (Grand Rapids, Zondervan, 2009)

KINDLE BOOKS

St Augustine, *The Confessions of Saint Augustine* (Translated by E.B. Pusey, Kindle Book)

Peter De Rosa, *Vicars of Christ, The Dark Side of the Papacy* (Kindle)

Thomas P. Doyle A.W. Richard Sipe and Patrick J. Wall, *Sex, Priests and Secret Codes, The Catholic Church's 2000-Year Paper Trail of Sexual Abuse* (Kindle)

Justin Humphreys (Author) Lisa Oakley (Author), *Escaping the Maze of Spiritual Abuse: Creating Healthy Christian Cultures* (Kindle)

Dr Steven D. Jenkins, *From Pentecost to the Pentecostal Movement* (Kindle)

Hans Kung, *The Catholic Church: A Short History (Universal History)* (Kindle, 2006)

T.E. Lawrence, *The Seven Pillars of Wisdom,* 1926 (Kindle)

Henry C Lea, *An Historical Sketch of Sacerdotal Celibacy in the Christian Church* (Kindle)

Ian Maxwell, *Everyday Life in 19th Century Ireland* (Kindle)

Asenath Nicholson, *Annals of the Famine in Ireland* (Books Ulster, 2017, Kindle)

John Maxwell, *The Five Levels of Leadership, Proven Steps to Maximise your Potential* (Kindle)

John O'Donoghue, *Eternal Echoes: Celtic Reflections on Our Yearning to Belong* (Kindle)

A. W. Richard Sipe, *Celibacy in Crisis: A Secret World Revisited* (Brunner-Routledge, 2003, Kindle)

ON-LINE ARTICLES

A Lutheran Layman, *Martin Luther, 'Celibacy Is Contrary to Nature'* http://www.lutheranlayman.com/2015/07/martin-luther-celibacy-is-contrary-to.html

Augustine's view of Sexuality https://www.cliffsnotes.com/literature/s/st-augustines-confessions/critical-essays/augustines-view-of-sexuality

His Majesty's Commissioners for Inquiring into The Condition of The Poorer Classes in Ireland, With Appendix (A.) And Supplement, digitised by the University of Southampton Library Digitisation Unit https://archive.org/stream/op1245191-1001/op1245191-1001_djvu.txt, 8 July 1835

Nathan Busenitz, *Did the Early Church Teach Transubstantiation?* April 21, 2016, https://blog.tms.edu/did-the-early-church-teach-transubstantiation

James Davis, *Core Faith: Understanding the Essentials of The Christian Life. lesson Six: Principles of Biblical Interpretation* https://bible.org/seriespage/lesson-6-principles-biblical-interpretation

Martin Luther, *Open Letter to the Christian Nobility of the German Nation Concerning the Reform of the Christian Estate* https://web.stanford.edu/~-jsabol/certainty/readings/Luther-ChristianNobility.pdf, 1520

Martin Luther, *An Open Letter to The Christian Nobility*, (Project Wittenberg) https://christian.net/pub/resources/text/wittenberg/luther/web/nblty-05.html

Thomas O'Loughlin, *The Catholic Church and Celibacy: An Approach from Historical*

Theology (The Japan Mission Journal, 2013) https://nottingham-repository.worktribe.com/OutputFile/1315852

Stephen Greenblatt, *How St. Augustine Invented Sex*, (The New Yorker 2017) https://www.newyorker.com/magazine/2017/06/19/how-st-augustine-invented-sex

John Oates, *Why did celibacy become mandatory for priests?* https://evidenceforchristianity.org/why-did-celibacy-become-mandatory-for-priestsr/

John Oates, *What happened in early Christianity between A.D 180-311?* https://evidenceforchristianity.org/what-happened-in-early-christianity-between-a-d-180-311r/

Helen L. Owen, *When Did the Catholic Church Decide Priests Should Be Celibate?* https://historynewsnetwork.org/aoptionrticle/696

The Wives of Clergy in the 12th Century, copied from the Vatican II mail list
https://womenpriests.org/sexuality/wives-the-wives-of-clergy-in-the-12th-century/

John White and Steven Ozment, *Christianity and Family Law An Introduction*
https://www.researchgate.net/publication/334707663_Martin_Luther
(Cambridge, Cambridge University Press 2017)

Gary Wills, *Apostolic Transgression*
https://www.nytimes.com/2013/02/17/books/review/why-priests-by-garry-wills.html?referringSource=articleShare

PERIODIC

David S Burns, *The Perfectionist's Script for self-Defeat*, Psychology Today
(N.Y., November 1980)

Dublin Correspondent, *Irish Eviction Scenes* (London The Daily Telegraph,
1887)

W Dayton Roberts, *Liberation Theologies* (Christianity Today, 17 May 1985)

What is the Baptism of the Holy Ghost and Fire? (Flames of Fire. No 1.
October 1911)

The Baptism in the Holy Ghost. A Distinction (Flames of Fire, No. 7. October
1912)

How to receive the Baptism in the Holy Ghost and Fire (Flames of Fire, No.
34, January 1916)

James Goff, *Charles Parham's Endtime Revival, The Eschatological Expectations of Tongue Speech in Early Pentecostalism* (November 10-12, 1988,
Springfield, Missouri, The Flower Pentecostal Heritage Centre Archives)

Séamus Murphy SJ, *Dark Liturgy, Bloody Praxis: The 1916 Rising* (Studies, spring 2016, Volume 105, Number 417)

Desmond O'Donnell, *Celibacy* (Maynooth, The Furrow, February 1972)

Agnes Ozman, *The First One to Speak in Tongues* (The Latter Rain Evangel, January 1909)

Max Turner, *Tongues An Experience for all in the Pauline Churches* (Asian Journal of Pentecostal Studies, August 1998)

Ronald Walls, *Celibacy and the Priesthood* (Maynooth, The Furrow, 2003).

"Don't let the noise of other's opinions drown out your own inner voice"

ABOUTH THE AUTHOR

After eight years of training as a Catholic priest, Mike Phillips was ordained in 1977 and served as a missionary priest for six years, three of which were spent in Ghana, West Africa. He left the priesthood in 1983 to train as a secondary school teacher. After fourteen years in education, he returned to full-time ministry in a Pentecostal church, where he has spent the last twenty-five years. He is currently semi-retired and serves as associate minister in the church he planted. He is currently involved in planting another church. His qualifications include a BA in Languages and a BD in Theology, both from St Patrick's college, Maynooth. He gained a Post Graduate Certificate in Education (PGCE) in 1984 and graduated from St John's College, Nottingham in 2003 with a MA in Mission and Ministry.

Milton Keynes UK
Ingram Content Group UK Ltd.
UKHW011105220823
427155UK00005BA/133